P9-DNQ-592

Dying We Live

We are treated as unknown and yet well known; as dying, and behold we live…as sorrowful, yet always rejoicing; as poor, yet making many rich; as having nothing, yet possessing everything.

2 Corinthians 6: 8-9

Also by Edward S. Gleason

Redeeming Marriage

DYING
WE
LIVE

Edward S. Gleason

COWLEY PUBLICATIONS
Cambridge, Massachusetts

Published in the United States
of America by Cowley Publications, a
division of the Society of St. John the Evangelist. No por-
tion of this book may be reproduced, stored in or intro-
duced into a retrieval system, or transmitted, in any form
or by any means, including photocopying, without the
prior written permission of Cowley Publications, except in the case of brief
quotations embodied in critical
articles and reviews.

International Standard Book Number
1-56101-014-6
Library of Congress Number
90-36006

Cover design by Linda A. Bachert
Cover photograph by Vernon Sigl

Library of Congress Cataloging-in-Publication Data

Gleason, Edward S., 1933–
Dying we live / Edward S. Gleason.
p. cm.
Includes bibliographical references.
ISBN 1-56101-014-6 (acid-free)
1. Episcopal Church. Burial of the dead. 2. Episcopal Church. Holy Eucharist.
3. Consolation. 4. Death—Religious aspects—Christianity. 5. Episcopal
Church—Doctrines. 6. Episcopal Church—Liturgy. 7. Anglican Communion—
Doctrines. 8. Anglican Communion—Liturgy. I. Title.
BX5947.B9G42 1990
264'.030985—dc20   90-36006

This book is printed on acid-free paper and was produced
in the United States of America.

Cowley Publications
980 Memorial Drive
Cambridge, Massachusetts 02138

*For my
father and mother
Gay and Winifred
who brought me to life
and through their deaths
opened the window to
ever larger life*

Acknowledgments

THE DREAM TO WRITE was awakened in me when, as a boy, my father took me again and again to Fenway Park to see Ted Williams hit a home run. The Red Sox almost always lost, but Williams often hit the home run. On the way home, at dinner, and again through the following week, my father would say to me: "Ted Williams may not be a gifted fielder, nor tip his hat to the crowd, but he hits better than anyone of this or any time. He'll always find a place on any team. The gift I wish for you is the ability to write. Learn to write, and write and write and write again, and there will always be a place for you to do what matters."

Under his tutelage, and then guided by others, I wrote many different words. Always it was clear, however, what I sought, as the expression of the love my father invested in me, was to write a book, to become an author.

Well past the age of fifty, I was still a writer, not an author. Then I met Cynthia Shattuck. To her are offered thanks and praise, for she believed that I could become an author.

E. S. G.

Conversion of St. Paul 1990
Alexandria, Virginia

Table Of Contents

Dying We Live

Prologue

CHARLES STIRRED. THE NIGHT had been filled with dreams. The curtains at the east window were beginning to be framed by gray morning light; the dreams remained, jumbling together past and present and a hint of the future. Through it all, the threat of grief. Instinctively he reached out to draw her to him and realized they had been sleeping in an embrace and was reassured that the present would, at least for now, forestall the future.

Nancy slept on, her face serene. As he raised himself on his left elbow and looked down at her, his remembered dreams took on a pattern. He saw himself in his parents' house, their bedroom, and then the bedroom of his childhood. Nancy was there with the entire family; he was particularly aware of the presence of all their grown children. They talked and laughed in that house of dreams of shared events and past times that again became vivid and colorful: comings and goings, trips, endings, graduations, departures, separations, weddings, moves, deaths, illness, recovery.

The memories were full—the stuff that bound them together and made them a family. Then, too often, the recurring taste of unresolved pain, lingering sorrow. Gathered in their circle of love, clearly both their beginning and their fulfillment, grief dominated, unanswered and ominous.

Then Charles was wide awake, and the dreams gone. He realized that on this day, or some day in the future no different from this one, he would know his ultimate

1

grief. She would be dead, and he alone. Children, friends, counselors, priest—none would ever replace her face, her love, her presence.

What purpose, he wondered, in planting the garden, if not to see her face when the job was complete? Why plan a trip or cook a meal or read a book or write a letter or open a bottle of wine, if not to share it with her? Every word, every act was an adventure, an act of love, when she was present. Without her nothing would make sense.

He found that when he wrote to one of his friends after the death of a husband or wife, words made no difference. Did it matter that he cared? What could sustain someone in the face of such loss? It was more than the death of the best part of you. It was the death of perspective and hope.

When the time came, he knew he would be brave, but no other person could ever be flesh of his flesh, life of his life. If death happened to one of them, it happened to both. Marriage was a bond stronger than anything else— except death.

Death happens. A house is not a home, only the place we live for awhile. No job is for a lifetime, only a way to fill some of our days. Friendships end when interests shift or the moving van arrives. No revolution, however passionate, ever really changed the world, only the roles and players. The dream dies; the vision fades. We move and change. All flesh is grass. In the midst of life we are in death. Sooner or later, everything ends.

This realization had gathered grief in his early morning dreams of familiar places and people, fueled by memories of his many losses. These had roused him to the knowledge that the love they clung to must also one day end. When this happened, when this terror struck, grief would again raise him up as it had in the past. It must. Grief leads to new life.

He wanted to talk, as they often did at daybreak. He spoke her name. She did not reply. He spoke again. She stirred, and without words, welcomed his caress. He wanted to ask her, "Is love more powerful than death?" Close as he had come, he had never dared, not in all their years of marriage. Nor did he ask her now; she was asleep, and then so was he.

         ॠ   ॠ   ॠ

He stood by the still-open grave. Everything had ended, and he remained alone to complete the ritual of burial. The first few shovels were the most painful. The rocks and clay, residue of a primordial sea, struck the wooden box each time with the hollow sound of a wrecking ball and evoked images of what lay inside, her body that once lived and breathed and loved. Three men dressed in yellow slickers watched. When he finished, they moved forward to replace the sod. He stood for a while before turning to leave. It was over.

As it turned out, it had only just begun.

Death Happens 🍁

THE WORDS HE SPOKE at his college commencement were repeated a few weeks later at his funeral. "A friend of mine once asked me, 'How does leukemia feel—is it like a cold?' It sounds stupid, but she was not far off...I started thinking what it would be like to die at twenty. I cried hard, but not for the jobs I would never have, nor for the money I was not going to make, not even for the degree I was never going to receive. On that day I thought of the many wonderful friends I had had and the chance that I would never see them again. I thought of my family. It was love I cried for that day. I wanted to reach out and hold hands with everyone I had ever known.

"Then I thought of how I had lived. I thought of how many friendships I had let dissolve because I did not have enough time for them. I thought of the day-to-day obsessions I had let interfere with love. I thought of the pace I had set for myself, never taking time to be—just be. I thought that if I died that summer I might never have lived. And yes, I felt cold.

"I vowed I would get up and fight the leukemia again just to have the chance to slow down and to love. There is nothing more important or more powerful. Every two weeks I go back to the cancer hospital, and I see and hear tremendous suffering. But the suffering is smothered by enduring love and fearless love. I go there, and I am reminded there is a reason why we are all here, a reason why we put up with this world of ours.

"If we just take the time to remember, we don't have to forget each other."

ଧ   ଧ   ଧ

Death happens, despite what we do to avoid it. Everything that begins, ends. The fact may not be welcome, but it is realistic. Death is a central part of life, and despite everything it takes from us, so too it enriches and strengthens.

ଧ   ଧ   ଧ

...The entire family had gone together to the circus—Barnum and Bailey—and sat in the very first row of the Coliseum. Right down on the floor, next to the main runway, she could almost reach down and touch the fuzzy red hair of her favorite clown.

Scared when the elephants came out, eighteen of them, lined up so close you could touch them, she held her breath and prayed nothing would happen. It didn't. They all laughed when the clowns erupted from the little car, and she and her father held hands while the couple walked the high wire. When it was all over, none of them was ready to go home, and they walked through sideshows. Daddy bought her a chameleon in a little pasteboard box that looked like an ice cream container.

Running through the front door and down the hall, she put the chameleon in an old glass aquarium and placed it on her bedside table. The next morning, a sunny May day with the promise of warmth in the air, she said, "Good morning," and named him Tony. At breakfast she and her sister decided to play house on the front lawn and set up a card table covered with the green and red cloth that Aunt Eleanor had given them at Christmas. The two of them crawled in underneath.

After making themselves cozy and deciding where each doll belonged, she ran in to get Tony. The old aquarium wasn't right for outdoors, so she found an empty peanut butter jar stored under the sink, lifted Tony by the tail into the jar, screwed on the lid, carried him outside, and placed him next to her favorite doll, Tina.

Tony and Tina made a perfect couple. It was time for tea. Tina's was just pretend, but Tony received freshly picked grass, placed in his jar, right next to his head, where it would be handy to eat. Just then their mother called them to lunch. "Leave everything right there. You can go back after your nap."

It was mid-afternoon when she opened her eyes and stared right into the aquarium. Tony wasn't there! Then she remembered, and jumped up to go and find him in the house with Tina. She crawled over to the corner and picked up the bottle. Tony was lying on his back, motionless. She couldn't believe it, unscrewed the jar, put in two fingers, turned him over and rubbed him on his back. Then she smelled the onion grass, and it took her breath away. Tony felt stiff. Something was wrong. Holding the uncovered jar, with the greatest of care, she crawled out, backward, stood up, and turned and looked into her mother's face.

Slowly, the child became ashen, then flushed, and shaking all over, started to cry. The two sat together on the grass, arms around each other, rocking back and forth Both knew there was nothing to do, nothing at all. Tony was dead.

That was her first time.

❧   ❧   ❧

Everyone has a first time for experiencing death, a time remembered, unless it is so painful, so dreadful, or happens so early in life that we have pushed it back into some dark recess of our mind. Most first times are not as stirring or poignant as the child John Kennedy saluting his father's casket. It may be very undramatic. Death is daily, even hum-drum, and we are never prepared to anticipate it.

Death happens, and it strikes us unawares. The chameleon, the kitten caught by a vicious dog, the puppy who runs too quickly across the street, perhaps even the grandmother who comes to visit and never wakes up early one morning, down the hall in the spare room. That is how death happens.

Then there are questions, questions about responsibility, guilt, pain, involvement. Questions, always questions. Questions like: "So what? What does it mean? Wouldn't it have been better if we had never met, then there couldn't be any pain, could there? Better if I had not bothered, not cared? Why did I allow myself to love?"

That is how death happens. In the midst of life we are in death. Even as life begins, so too does the road to death. Whatever we value, whatever we love—a person, a marriage, a place, a job, a pet, a favorite book, a view, a house—will be taken from us. We remember and relive, again and again, the first moment of such loss. That same moment will be repeated. Such moments remain, forever, until our own death. Each time death happens, the inevitable reality of loss and pain is etched into our being, deeper and deeper. We live it and relive it, come to know it as an intimate partner and companion. Not as a friend, death is never a friend, but it is closer to us than breathing, nearer than hands and feet.

What did the mother say as she rocked her sobbing daughter on the grass that warm May afternoon? Did she tell a lie, and say, "Everything is going to be all right"? Did she say, "You didn't mean to put the onion grass in the bottle"? Or did she speak the truth? "In life we are in death. It is a fact, one we learn again and again, and one you have begun to learn. Let us hold one another tight and remember that even as there is death, so too there is love, and love is stronger than death."

Death may not happen every day, but many, many times in our lifetime. There is no other choice. When it happens, what do we say? Or think? To whom do we turn? What do we do? We have to do something. Is it just being there that matters most? That's a beginning. We feel useless. Death hurts. It really hurts. Make it go away. Why did this happen? There must be some mistake.

No, there is no mistake. Death happens. When it happens, we join hands, literally and figuratively, with those whom we love, those who have loved us. Dumbstruck, struck down, we can not just stand there, and so we bind ourselves to one another.

&a.   &a.   &a.

9

...Looking to renew an old friendship with the rector, I wandered into the coffee hour of a large downtown church at noon on a winter Sunday. A kindly older woman, walking with a cane and wearing a hat, noticed I was alone. She approached me and asked, "So, what's your name?" I responded, she told me hers, and then volunteered with warmth and cheer: "You want to know what this church is? I'll tell you. It's love. That's what it is. My husband of more than fifty years died unexpectedly two years ago, and for an entire year I never cooked a single meal. These people, the people of this parish, gathered around me and fed me, every single day for one whole year. That's love, and that's what this church is all about."

இ   இ   இ

God is made known in human life through the cross. We know God first through Jesus, whose cross is continually present in our daily experience. The cross of Jesus is every experience of death and loss, disappointment and defeat.

The cross is also much more. It is Easter and victory and release and new life, all of those things. But at the very first the cross is for us as it was for Jesus' closest friends and followers on that Good Friday afternoon when they took his limp and bloodied body down from the cross. They knew nothing of Easter, not then. They had never heard of St. Paul's letters, words that had not yet been written. All those few remaining faithful knew was that this cross had hurt them, deeply and personally. This cross forced them to know with certainty that there was no hope. There was only pain and death. They had known Jesus as a living, breathing man, their friend and leader. Now he was dead. As the pain of this death, proclaimed by the cross, became part of them, fully and finally, then they came to know the Lord.

This is what the cross means, every single time we look at it. If God would find us, it will happen through death or not at all. The cross towers over and pervades all of life. But whenever possible, we avoid everything that the cross means. Even though this is impossible, we invent every means to believe that life may be lived without struggle and pain and loss: without the cross. The inescapable fact remains. God is made known in human life through the cross.

Without death, there is no life, and so it is that in dying we live.

                    ❧   ❧   ❧

...Far in the distance a clock struck two. He had not yet fallen asleep. There was good reason. He turned over to find a more comfortable position, but it was no use. Every little incident of the day, not to mention all the bigger and seemingly impossible concerns of his new job, kept pouring in upon him, threatening to crush him. What was the point? The job was overwhelming. He turned again, this time to lie flat on his back, stared at the ceiling, and said aloud, "This job is going to kill me."

Right then, he had a vision. Maybe it was just common sense, but someone said, or he heard, or he knew, that this was the point, the whole point. If your job or your marriage or your friendship or something central and important doesn't kill you, then there is no possible reason for being alive. From the moment of birth we are going to die. That's fact. We may embrace that fact in the name of God. We want to avoid it, either to deny the future or to jump into it, but first we face death. There is one way of saying yes and many ways of saying no. The choice is always ours.

Once we own up to death, grief is the process by which the losses of death are transformed into new life. It is a process we all frequently experience, every day and in small ways. It is an experience we have known from childhood. The experience is always unwelcome, but the process is consistent. When the time comes, sooner or later, when we face grief, it is always as it was for that unknown friend wearing a hat in the downtown parish. Grief is the process by which loss is transformed into new life.

When death happens, we join hands with those who know our pain most deeply. We meet them in many places, but when death happens, we have the opportunity to meet them first as the church, gathered together for the church's statement at the time of death, the Burial of the Dead in the Book of Common Prayer. Here we are united to our roots and the depths of our faith, gathered with those who love us, those alive and those long dead. Loss draws us into a band of friends, family, and lovers to face death with us and to surround us with a cloud of witnesses. In the center of that band, the cross proclaims, is Jesus the Christ, who died so that through death, we might be given new life.

Once death happens, we have no choice but to face it. The choice is not welcome, but there is no way to turn away, and if we do not turn away, then we may be strengthened by the common experience of this rite of burial, which brings to our loss the perspective of countless generations. We begin by acknowledging that loss, deep and painful, as the very title of the liturgy makes clear: The Burial of the Dead. We gather to bury the dead and to face together the reality of death.

This book proclaims that conviction. It is a book written for each of us who knows death, and that is every one of us. We are all scared of death, we run from it, make fun of it, wish we knew how to make sense of it. We never shall until we experience it, and then we discover that we have known that experience all along. The gospel has much to say to our experience of death. The process of reflection that we undertake is not easy. No one wants to think seriously and logically about death; we prefer a salve, something that will cover it up. But we know from the Christian faith and the rite of burial that we came into the world to die. We shall know death many times and in many forms. To live is to die, again and again, until we draw our final breath. But now, as then, it is only in dying that, behold, we live.

I Am Resurrection

The Opening Anthems

THE STREET WAS FLOODED with morning sunlight, and it made the darkness of the church overwhelming. Waiting for his eyes to adjust, Charles noticed the smell—old and stale, reminiscent of dust and disuse. Everything seemed forgotten, left over, and he wanted to turn and go, return to the sunlight. Instead he stood, rooted to the floor, trapped. The moment he had most dreaded during his whole life was finally his, alone.

Three short days ago he had heard her call, "Come and have breakfast." While she made the coffee and he had cooked the oatmeal, they spoke of the previous evening, his dinner meeting, her visit with their eldest daughter and new baby. Sitting together, looking out at the garden drenched from evening showers, they shared plans for the day. Nancy first to the office, then lunch with an old friend thirty miles into the country, and back to see a client. Charles would hold office hours for section leaders, then do some writing in the library, and teach in the late afternoon. The evening they would spend at home alone together.

They kissed good-bye at the kitchen door. "I love you more and more," he called after her as he watched her vanish towards her car, and then turned to his study.

Her lunch with the college roommate had been delicious, talk spanning all those years. There was so much to share that she never noticed the heavy rain. She left at two-thirty, full of happy memories, looking ahead to the evening with Charles, oblivious to the weather, the complete lack of visibility, the stop sign in the center of town, the concrete truck that hit her, full force, at thirty miles an hour, directly at the driver's door. Charles never saw her again.

When he finally returned home in the early dark, the house was empty even though it was well past the hour she meant to return. No doubt she had changed her plan. Nancy was given to last-minute whims. The telephone rang. He turned with a start, longing to hear her voice, and ran to the phone, hearing her say again, "Come and have breakfast." It was Nancy's college roommate.

Her voice broke even as she began to speak, and in an instant he knew it all. His worst fantasy had come true. "Charles," she said, "Charles. I don't know how to tell you. There's been an accident...Nancy...she couldn't have felt a thing...it happened so fast."

The voice stopped talking. Charles could think of nothing to say. After what seemed like a long time, he heard, "Charles, Charles, are you still there?"

That had been three days ago.

His eyes were now accustomed to the dark of the still-empty church. He had arrived early to sit alone in the second pew, where they had been so often together, wait for the burial to begin, and listen for the one voice that might have something to say. All the tender expressions of sorrow and support from his family and neighbors that had filled the past three days were honest and heartfelt, but none penetrated the thick insulation that protected him from his feelings. Life had gone.

Staring blankly ahead, numb and alone, he wondered how he would get through this day. The whole business was barbaric. Nancy was dead. Wouldn't he be better off if he could just forget the whole thing and get back to living? Only he hadn't been able to do anything, not a thing except think about Nancy.

His eyes fixed on the cross on the altar. It was just an object, a symbol, but if he could concentrate on it, since it was there anyway, it might take his mind off Nancy. Charles focused every ounce of his available energy on the cross. He was with the cross, and with him who had chosen it. Jesus had died on that cross, and when that happened, God became present in a completely new way.

He was aware that for several minutes now the church had begun to fill. There were noises, scuffling, the mumble of many voices. For the longest time he continued to stare straight ahead, afraid to look around, afraid of what and who he would see, and how he would feel. And so he didn't. He hadn't asked any of them to come, no one, except the children, and as soon as he thought of them they were there, slipping into the pew alongside him. He knew that the one moment he had most dreaded had arrived, and he turned to see strangers and confusion at the door, her casket, covered in white, being rolled in, a cross, a priest, others, all coming towards him.

The great square mahogany box rolled slowly, soundlessly down the aisle, around it his two brothers, Nancy's brother, his college roommate, not one of them looking

17

like themselves. He smiled secretly remembering how Nancy so often had referred to "her pallbearers." Well, there they were, but there was nothing funny about them.

Then there were words.

I am Resurrection and I am Life, says the Lord.

The pattern of our lives dictates that as soon as we are born, we begin to die. What quickens our breath and our bodies too soon begins to wind down, our powers mental and physical gradually, and then quite perceptibly, diminish.

The great gift of the Christian heritage is that when death happens, we gather with those we love and who love us in the assurance of the resurrection, to hear these words proclaim that this is not all there is. The purpose of life is more than this great darkened room called a church, muffled voices, and a pervasive sense of gloom and sorrow at the end. There is more: resurrection and life.

We are brought together by the Book of Common Prayer to celebrate the Burial of the Dead. The facts of life and death occasion this meeting and created this place. We are gathered together here, in the sight of God and in the face of this company, to honor a life and mark a death. We shall all die—many times. Death is more than the one-time event that occasions our longest journey. Death is a daily companion. Death is confronted in the senseless loss of a woman who ran a stop sign on a rainy day, but death is also the inevitable result of every undertaking. Sooner or later, life is never a win-win situation; life involves loss. The question is, how do we deal with the loss? Is loss to be all we know, or will there be more?

Whoever has faith in me shall have life,
even though he die.

...When she was still a very little girl, more than anything else she loved to go roller skating. That didn't happen too often, since her mother didn't have that much time or extra money to spare, but there were birthday parties, special times, when she almost flew around the big concrete oval. She began to try out fancy moves that seemed easy, natural; people even backed away to watch.

A pretty lady who watched with special care skated alongside her. "It's a joy to watch you. Have you ever skated on ice?"

"Oh, no. I lie awake nights and dream about it, but it's only a dream."

"Perhaps not. Let's go talk to your mother."

That was how it began. She often looked back and thought that it seemed impossible—a miracle. The miracle involved countless hours of effort, practice, expense, sacrifice on the part of mother and daughter. The early morning hours driving to practice brought a closeness few mothers and daughters experience. Progress, recognition, one successful competition after another, made it all worthwhile, or so it seemed.

She grew up, finished high school, won a scholarship to a good college. She was bright enough, but the figure skating helped. Now a national figure, the little roller skater was headed toward the Olympics. When she looked back much later, from the perspective of middle age, it was all a blur of single-minded devotion, long practices, the attempt to keep up in college, continuous competitions, and then that moment when it all came down to one final event. She had done everything right, and she was poised to become the winner.

Something went wrong at the very beginning. The stage was set: expectation, bright lights, a crowd, huge and enthusiastic. She took her stance, the music began, but it was wrong, all wrong. The first triple jump failed. If this had been a practice she would have started all over again, but here she had to go on. None of her flair, style, competence was there. It wasn't working. Why? No explanation. Every undertaking once begun must some-time end. This was the night when her figure-skating career would come to an end. Before thousands of watch-ful and expectant eyes, she experienced the death that awaits all athletes.

Yet at the moment she stepped from the ice, something happened. This death she would carry with her, always and forever, but right then she was raised up to know that her future had opened to her in a new and mysteri-ous way. Always, even when she was very little, her dearest dream had been to be a doctor. This was the dream that had brought her to college, not the life of a figure skater. Skating was now behind her, and new life could begin.

And everyone who has life,
and has committed himself to me in faith,
shall not die forever.

...When she was five, she ran away from home and hid in the snowbank by the barberry bushes at the foot of the road. Her father came looking for her, calling and calling, and when she finally came out to him, his face was streaming with tears.

He ran toward her, stumbling as he came, bent over and snatched her up and hugged her, hugged her so hard she thought he would stop her breathing.

"I love you. I love you. I love you," he said to her over and over again, his tears continuing to flow. "But don't run away. Never run away. We have so little time, and so much that we must do before it is too late."

As for me, I know that my Redeemer lives
and that at the last he will stand upon the earth.
After my awaking, he will raise me up;
and in my body I shall see God.
I myself shall see, and my eyes behold him
who is my friend and not a stranger.

These familiar words from the Book of Job are as well known as any in the Bible. In the midst of a life and a compelling drama told in poetic form, after a series of the most demanding trials, losses, deaths, and long before the drama concludes, Job utters this emphatic statement of unswerving trust and hope in God despite all losses and disappointments.

The "redeemer" in Hebrew tradition was most often a family member with the legal obligation to buy back or "redeem" a relative who had been sold into slavery. For St. Paul it became a metaphor: God redeems men and women from the slavery of sin and death. For Job, this was not the case, for no family member remained to redeem him. In the midst of trial, however, Job looks beyond tradition, the known and acceptable, to the conviction that he will see God, that death will not be the end, and that he will be brought at last before the very face of the divine.

Such a conviction is rooted in the very being of a person. There is the rare and unusual person, we are told, for whom this has always been true. "Once-born" knowledge of the Lord is part of them even from birth. God said to the prophet Jeremiah, "Before I formed you in the womb I knew you, and before you were born I consecrated you." But such people are rare. Most are more apt to be like you and me. Knowledge is not given, but grows through experience that may have happened all at once or through a series of events, not unlike the deepening realization of love binding together two people in a close friendship or a man and woman in marriage. It is something that happens, given as a gift. We need to be open, to watch and wait, listen and pray, just as we must be at the right time and place to be met by the one whom we shall befriend or marry. We can not make it happen.

Is faith involved? By all means! The conviction that our Redeemer lives is a gift of grace, but it does not take root and grow unless openness and willingness make it possible. We are always free to cast our faith away; to turn away from God, to be alone, to die alone. This opportunity is precisely parallel to the choice that some people make to allow a friendship to die, or to break their marriage vows by starting an affair.

&.   &.   &.

...For twenty-two years she devoted herself totally, all there was of her life, to him and to the three children. It happened on a Sunday afternoon when he returned

22

home sometime before six, after spending his entire day working in the office.

She was in the kitchen peeling carrots when the front door opened and closed. But he never appeared. After a while, she wiped her hands on her apron and walked out through the dining room, calling for him. No answer. Slowly, she went up the stairs and found him in the back room bending over a suitcase that was almost full. When she asked what he was doing, still he did not speak. Not until he closed the suitcase, lifted it from the chair, and turned to face her. "I'm leaving, Fran. Right now, I'm leaving." He started to say something more, didn't, picked up the suitcase, walked past her, and down the stairs.

Long afterward she thought wryly that it was just like an early afternoon soap opera. For now, she collapsed into the chair from which he had just lifted the suitcase and sighed. Then she heard a car start. She stood up with great pain and reached the window just in time to see his car disappear.

Twenty-two years. For what? So that he could walk out with that little bitch from his office? She could already hear her mother trying to tell her that time heals all wounds. Not true. She had been used. Time wouldn't make a difference. Nothing would make a difference. She had been good and kind and faithful and true and that didn't matter a bit, not one single bit.

🐺 🐺 🐺

Job's faith came only after trial and unswerving loyalty and response to his vision of God. The end of life greets us as a gift, but what happens through and beyond death is not automatic. It is rooted in faithfulness. We may change the course at any time.

For none of us has life in himself,
and none becomes his own master when he dies.
For if we have life, we are alive in the Lord,
and if we die, we die in the Lord.
So, then, whether we live or die,
we are the Lord's.

The American people and culture, created in a wilderness, forged by a revolution and continually influenced by a frontier mentality, as our people kept pushing, pushing their limits ever westward, holds steadfastly to the belief that we find life and its meaning only in ourselves and nowhere else. Grace—the free and undeserved gift received from another, from God—is not really part of what we expect. Luck may exist, but after all, we tell ourselves, God helps those who help themselves.

The natural corollary of this deep conviction is that death really does not exist. Life is to be prolonged at all costs—as long as the ill and elderly are safely removed from sight. When death does occur, then it is to be denied, and vast commercial enterprises have developed to reinforce and undergird this denial. This denial has brought into being not only nursing homes and retirement villages, but the life insurance industry created to make the continuation of life possible. Life will go on just as if you or I were still present; the insurance provides for my absence. The denial of death, central to our understanding of life, is supported by every means available.

಄   ಄   ಄

...When he got to the open casket, he cringed. The body that lay there, wearing her own clothes and still bearing some resemblance to the person he once knew, had nothing whatever to do with the woman who had been flesh of his flesh, life of his life for twenty-five years. It looked like a mannequin, made up from powder and plastic, silent and cold.

Still he could not help standing next to it for the longest time, gazing down and wishing, hoping, praying, that she would suddenly rise up. He studied the breast, so still, and his eyes played tricks on him, wanting him to believe that it did rise and fall, rhythmically, regularly. Only it did not. She was dead, and this thing, this body, was an obscenity, an insult, a nothing. She was dead, and what lay before him, apparently so nearly alive, could not change that fact. This was not the beloved woman, the one with whom he had shared a life, created children, felt joy and pain, love and release. This person was gone. He was alone.

He turned and never looked in the casket again.

          ая   ая   ая

...The young man had just turned eighteen, graduated from high school last month and was headed for college. He was sitting in the passenger seat coming home from the basketball game when the driver lost control and careened off a telephone pole, breaking it in half exactly where he was sitting.

The visiting hours were lengthy and crowded. His casket was open, a small prie-dieu placed adjacent to the great bronze box in which his body lay. He looked as alive as on his graduation day, only he was wearing the suggestion of a smile and his warm-up jacket with school insignia proudly displayed on his left breast.

              ❧   ❧   ❧

Death is denied by our use of language, most especially in the frequent avoidance of the word itself. One does not "die," one "passes." When life ends most persons speak not of "death" but of "passing," as if death were not the dramatic end of life, but merely a transition, a peaceful, pleasant passing. Death may sometimes be peaceful, but it is always a rupture, an ending, and it is unwelcome and painful.

              ❧   ❧   ❧

...Driving past the hospital on the outskirts of the city, coming in for dinner and an evening with some friends, we remembered that our dearest and oldest living friend, now ninety-two, lay sick there. We had been still newly married, one small baby and a second on the way, when Mrs. Fiske lived next door to us. She was best friend, confidante, mother, grandmother, counselor—all in one confident, straightforward Yankee woman of stature, grace and faith.

A quick U turn, back up High Street, into the parking lot, and we were at the front desk. "She's up on the second floor of the old north wing, N-221." The original part of the hospital showed more signs of age than we remembered, the lighting poor, making the whole space dingy on an early winter afternoon.

"I wonder if we could see Mrs. Fiske?" I asked of the nurse at the station in the midst of the corridor. Although

I had spoken clearly and slowly, she turned away as if I were invisible and she had not heard me.

"Do you think it might be possible for us to see Mrs. Fiske?" I inquired again. Still no response. The nurse became busy with paperwork and had now seated herself at her work space.

"Excuse me, but is Mrs. Fiske still on this wing?" This time the nurse looked up, put a finger over her mouth, and whispered, "She passed away, last night."

"She what?"

"She passed on."

"Well, is she still here?"

"No. She passed."

"You mean she died? Mrs. Fiske is dead?"

The nurse nodded. I walked to the end of the hall to the room where she had lain. The bed was empty, fresh and clean.

&ebd; &ebd; &ebd;

...That Saturday in the middle of May was a glorious spring day. The two of them, father and daughter, celebrated with a rare day in the city—shopping, the museum, lunch at a restaurant—all background to a long conversation about what had been going on in each of their lives, and what it all meant and where it was all heading.

Something compelled them to drive home on Huntington Avenue towards Brookline Village and Route One, and before realizing it they were abreast of the hospital, so they turned and went up the steep hill. "Let's stop by and see Beth."

Directed to a remote wing of the fifth floor of the hospital, they stepped from the elevator right into a gathering of nurses, all for that entire floor, clustered at the station located at the intersection of three corridors that stretched off in different directions. Father and daughter continued on and found the corridor absolutely deserted from one end to the other. More than half way down on the right, they came to Beth's room and knocked. Her husband opened the door and welcomed them.

He took each of them by the hand and over to the bed. Beth's breathing was slow, labored. She was in a coma, nearly gone. He spoke to her distinctly, loudly, lovingly, several times. Not a stir. "I guess she's asleep; she'll be so sorry to miss you. The two of us have been here alone all afternoon. Haven't even seen a sign of the nurses. Guess they're all busy."

We took one another's hands, prayed, let the silence seep into us, turned, and said goodbye. When we passed the nurses' station at the corner on the way to the elevator, they were all still huddled there.

           ❧   ❧   ❧

The chasm between life and death appears to be great, the gulf enormous, yet the distance is really imperceptible. What we perceive in this lifetime to be a great gap is only the blink of an eye. The rip in the fabric that is the distance between life and death is woven into one tapestry by the author and giver of life and of death: the Lord. The claim "Whether we live or die, we are the Lord's" begins with the realization that our death is an event of utter finality and continues with the terrible familiarity of separation as a time of pain. Then, and only then, we know that ending and separation bring new possibility, for we are held in death, even as we are held in life, by the Lord.

Happy from now on
are those who died in the Lord!
So it is, says the Spirit,
for they rest from their labors.

...Our last conversation took place the day before he died. The family had called and asked me to come, quickly, because he had asked to see me. It was time for a final talk, "What is next for Tim?" I had been chosen to talk to him about what would happen next to my old friend.

Even before hanging up the phone I could feel my body temperature rise, a reaction to grief, and for several hours I was ill. Physically, as well as in countless other ways, Tim resembled my father, who had been dead for thirty-three years. He and I had been close friends for a score of years. During four of them he had been my boss, a job he did not want but took on after I asked him. We held in common our deepest convictions: a personal faith in Jesus Christ, the importance of marriage, family, good education. Each of us was always present for the other at special family occasions.

After a long drive that began in the dark of early morning, I entered the back door at nine-thirty. His wife and daughter were sitting across the kitchen table, drinking coffee. The previous day had been a good one, they told me, too bad I couldn't have made it then. The night had not gone well. He was drained. Time was short, death near. But he knew I was coming. They told me that even if he was not able to speak, he could certainly nod.

The next I knew we were together in his bedroom, where Tim lay in a raised hospital bed. Without his glasses he looked wan and peaked, eyes closed, mouth open, oxygen tubes to the nose, hands crossed on his chest. I reached out and held his left hand and said hello. Eyes opened, smiled, twinkled. He seemed very much like Tim.

Before any words at all, his right hand came up, index finger extended—his hands were always big, but now the finger was especially long and gaunt—and his arm rose up from the bed, again and again and again, finger pointing upward, the words clear, strong: "I'm going to be with Him. I'm going to be with Him. I'm going to be with Him."

Then, as one motion and without pause, he turned his head toward the door, to the right, and with the same hand pointed, repeatedly, vigorously, emotionally, to the house beyond, the living room and kitchen where his wife sat. Words tumbled out of the power of love, of nearly fifty years of marriage. There was no question in his mind of the quality of life he and his wife had known and the new life that now waited "with Him."

When he spoke again, he asked of our new life in Virginia, "in the South," as he called it. Then quiet was followed by more conversation, his difficulty in swallowing. "What's the oxygen like?" "I wouldn't recommend it."

My pious words about the constant presence of death in all of life, weighed against Tim's lengthy knowledge of loss, seemed slight, almost insulting. Wondering if the pressure from my hand might be uncomfortable, I withdrew it, just as we began to talk of prayer. His right hand and arm reached out and grasped my entire arm, firmly, warmly. His whole personal presence and power began to overwhelm me, and I started to say goodbye. He looked straight at me, his eyes filling with tears, and said, "Kiss me," and drew me to him. We kissed. He said, "I love you." And I replied, "I love you too. Good bye." "Good bye," he said, "Good bye," as I turned and left the room, unable to see where I was going.

ಶಾ ಶಾ ಶಾ

This final opening anthem that speaks of "those who died in the Lord" is a biblical metaphor that sets before us a human perception, limited though it is, of the reality of Christian life beyond the grave. This perception rests upon our own experience on this side of the grave, translated, blown large, through the gates of death, into something new and different: the experience of eternal life.

Eternal life is the full experience of a distinct, often new, and only partially glimpsed moment of fullness and grace in the Lord. Granted, life beyond the grave is unknown until we experience it, and no one has yet returned to describe it, but we believe that it is somehow consistent with the lives we live now, lives that are given and lived in the Lord on this side of the grave. Death and resurrection are not abstract; they are here and now, a daily experience. Our experience of life in the Lord is happening now, not just when we die. We have known enough of the now, bits and snatches, glimpses, to be able to envision life eternal.

CHAPTER II

The Land of Light and Joy

The Collects

THE COFFIN HAD COMPLETED its journey down the center aisle to a resting place adjacent to Charles, who was standing at the end of the second pew. Nothing happened for some time except a lengthy silence immediately prior to the collects, the initial prayers to introduce the Bible readings. Her body was right next to him, close enough to touch but too far away to feel, and made him realize yet again that years ago, just after they were married, they had first openly acknowledged how much they depended on each other and always would.

Now, without warning or reason, she was gone. But it was not just that she had gone. The marriage was over as well. Once they had been three: Nancy, Charles, and their marriage. Two separate individuals bound together into a new creation that belonged to each, equally, and yet to neither one. This living and breathing creation drew its life from each of them, and when one died, the marriage died.

Now only he remained. Outside of their marriage no one else could understand what it was like to be Charles, twenty-five years married, so in love and now alone. He found it all very confusing: hollowness and pain mingled with the pure joy of memory, the memory of Nancy, and confusion was only one emotion. He was also bitter and angry, very angry. It just wasn't the right time for the marriage to be over, not nearly time. They had each known that it would come to this, that one would be taken and the other left. Sometimes they had talked about it, but then they had hoped against hope that if they had belonged to one another so long and so well, why should there ever be a time when this was not true? They ended such conversations knowing that when the time came....But the nagging doubt haunted each of them. That doubt had become a hollow, more than a hollow. Where once there had been so much, there was nothing.

Not quite nothing. He repeated her name over and over again, as if a prayer—Nancy, Nancy, Nancy, Nancy, Nancy, Nancy.

ᴁ   ᴁ   ᴁ

O God, whose mercies cannot be numbered: Accept our prayers on behalf of your servant N., and grant her (him) an entrance into the land of light and joy, in the fellowship of your saints; through Jesus Christ our Lord, who lives and reigns with you and the Holy Spirit, one God, now and for ever. Amen.

Mourning is the expression of grief, and the act of grief is powerful. If it is to empower, to bring us new life and not overpower us, then it must seek and find expression. Prayer for the dead is one such expression, the acknowledgment that just as the Lord loves each of us into being, so too when life on this earth comes to an end, then the dead continue to be enfolded by God's love. God, who loves both the living and the dead, is present for us in prayer, uniting us in God to the living and to the dead, the one whole fabric of God's creation.

The enfolding fabric of love that is God surrounds us, and we come to know it both in its presence and its absence.

ða.   ða.   ða.

...Her mother died when she was two, and she was sent to live with her grandmother while her father lived in Paris. "My father *sold* me" was how she explained it years later.

The grandmother was wonderful, the fulfillment of every little girl's dream, but it was not easy, growing up and knowing that both parents had abandoned her. More and more, she wondered if it had been her fault. Her mother died, she convinced herself, from a lingering illness brought on by childbirth. Then her father had fled— she decided he was unable to stand the sight of the murderer, his very own daughter.

She would dream of the mother she had hardly known, beautiful and distant, dressed in gowns that shimmered and trailed after her. She hoped, even prayed, that she would someday grow up to be the person her absent mother had been for her. In time grandmother wearied of answering her constant questions, her assumptions about mummy this and mummy that. Grandmother, too, felt deserted, put upon. It had never been her idea to spend her declining years raising yet another child, one who was unplanned and unwanted.

The child grew up knowing that she belonged to no one and wondering if she ever would.

❧　　❧　　❧

We come to pray for the dead. It is not an easy thing to do, for the dead have abandoned us. What we always feared most has happened, and we have been deserted, left alone. If we truly loved and were loved by she who is now dead, then we are in great pain; all we want is to have her back. If, on the other hand, our presence here is only to make a good appearance, then we are embarrassed to try to think of this person as one we loved, for we hardly knew her.

It may be that we only came here with the hope that when our turn comes, someone will show up. Someone might even say a prayer. How embarrassing if it came time to bury me and no one came!

But what prayer shall we offer on behalf of this dear friend? We can't have her back. She's gone. Shall we revive old memories, or imagine the words we should have spoken? Shall we pretend that she has not gone and left us? Might it be better to imagine her where she now is and think, for the very first time, of that time, nearer and nearer at hand, when again we shall be together? How will that be? Will she recognize me? Will she still love me?

It's lonely. You never should have gone and left me. Couldn't you have stayed just a while longer, so we could have talked it over? Then, perhaps we could have gone together. That's what friends are for, to be together. Now, it's lonely, cold, and dark. Probably you've forgotten already, forgotten those special times. Are you lonely? Why did you pick up so fast, with no warning, and leave?

         ی۔   ی۔   ی۔

...That hot summer in the inner-city hospital, the supervisor asked if Joe would spend some time with Margaret, the difficult one, the trouble-maker. On the top floor, at the end of the corridor, in the ward for those whose future was limited, at best. Their hours together turned out to be the most important part of the summer.

Margaret was born, grew up, and lived most of her life on the shores of Mobile Bay. During spring and summer, when the east wind blew for more than three days, right after heavy rains had swollen the rivers that fed the bay, then there was Jubilee, that extraordinary event when all life in the depths of the bay rose to the surface, flopping out on the shore for all to see and savour—flounder and crab and eels and sting rays by the hundreds and thousands.

This hot summer was Margaret's jubilee. From deep within her soul came every face she had ever known or ever been. The stories and faces came from everywhere, from deep underneath that dark and murky water came the beautiful and the painful. She would fasten her deep brown almond-shaped eyes directly on him, and she would talk of her past and all the things and people she had loved: her Mama and Papa and flowers and vegetables—all growing things—and cooking and drinking and smoking and telling stories.

One day, as they were talking, Margaret started to cry, and said, "I was never married to the man I lived with for those thirty-five years. He was a good man, and he loved me and my cooking too." She talked about Ed until he felt that the three of them, Margaret and Ed and Joe, had grown up together on the shores of Mobile Bay. Margaret went on. "Sometimes I used to go up there on the hill where he's buried and visit him. I lay down, right on top of him, right on his plot, and tell him how much I love him and how much I miss him. I carry him flowers. He loved flowers, you know."

Margaret smiled her beautiful smile, and Joe took both her hands. "Why don't we ask God to join us, and marry you and Ed, right here?" They did that, and when it was all over, Joe looked up. Tears ran down Margaret's face as the memories eased back below the surface. Margaret was very quiet, until she looked straight at him and said, "Thank you."

When the Burial of the Dead marks the death of a child, the situation has special poignancy.

O God, whose beloved Son took children into his arms and blessed them: Give us grace to entrust N., to your never-failing care and love, and bring us all to your heavenly kingdom; through Jesus Christ our Lord, who lives and reigns with you and the Holy Spirit, now and for ever. Amen.

We mourn the loss of promise, the unfulfilled and unrealized. We mourn, too, a reality that marks all of our lives.

Some people offer "comfort" at such a time by saying the ridiculous: "God loved her so much, dear thing, that he has called her home to be with Him." Such a statement, offered to explain a meaningless death that cut a future short, may mean well, but misses the point. It is also clearly untrue. When death occurs, the longing is ours and belongs to those who are left behind. Each of us belongs to God throughout all of time. Whether alive or dead, we are God's.

ða   ða   ða

...That summer his wife left him and took his two-year-old daughter. His only connection to his child was the weekly support check he wrote and her company on Saturdays from ten until six. Nothing in life had ever prepared him for the loss of his daughter.

Nothing in his lifetime had prepared him for loss, certainly not a loss as sudden and severe as this one. He knew he could do without his wife. Their brief so-called marriage had made it painfully clear that they had never known one another. Not when they had married and not now.

But the child, his daughter, she was different. From the morning he first saw her round little face, he had loved her. He had grown to love her more and more. She was his, the fruit of his loins, his joy and fulfillment, the heir to his own history and family. Now she was gone, or she might as well have been.

Saturdays were the worst and best part of the week. At the moment in the day when the two of them, father and child, began again to become comfortable with one another, it was time to put her in the car and drive the fourteen miles to the mother's house and leave her, not to see her again for another week—and lucky for that!

If they could just be together, not for hours, but days, weeks, the years for which he had planned so happily while lying in bed next to the pregnant woman who carried his child. Yes, damn it, his child!

That was bad enough, but something else was worse still. The child had become a myth, an event bigger than life, so big that it included an essential truth, true at all times and places. What happened between them, her and him, daughter and father, would happen to every person, event, moment, memory. From the moment anything begins, it is bound to end. His child had been born into this world only to be taken from him. All of life is loss.

When Wednesday came, he lived for Saturday. When Saturday came, he dreaded every moment until the terrible drive home in the dark. At least then he could be alone in peace and forget his loss.

❡ ❡ ❡

> . . . The majesty and burning of the child's death.
> I shall not murder
> The mankind of her going with a grave truth
> Nor blaspheme down the stations of the breath
> With any further
> Elegy of innocence and youth.
>
> Deep with the first dead lies London's daughter,
> Robed in the long friends,
> The grains beyond age, the dark veins of her mother,
> Secret by the unmourning water
> Of the riding Thames.
> After the first death, there is no other.

❡ ❡ ❡

...Arriving home from a short vacation late on a Saturday night, it came as a surprise to find the garage doors shut and locked. Was their daughter still out? They entered through a side door and found her car still running.

Their daughter was in the driver's seat, fallen to one side, no longer breathing. Her parents stood frozen in the garage, one on either side of the car, as paralyzed as their child's body had been by the carbon monoxide just before it was suffocated. Finally the father was able to reach in and turn the ignition key. They stood there, stupidly, with their eyes on her.

Why? Somehow no one had been able to tell this vulnerable young woman, full of such promise, that she was loved. The words had gotten caught in many different throats, or somehow they became twisted and came out all wrong. What she had heard, time and time again, was do more, be more, get better grades, make your mark, make us proud. Apparently she had felt that no matter what she did, she could never be good enough. Now the worst — what parents sometimes secretly fear but never speak of — had happened. How can life lose its meaning even before it has had a chance to happen?

When they couldn't stand there any longer, they walked in silence, single file, out of the garage and into the house. At the kitchen table they pulled up chairs and sat across from each other. He leaned his head on the table and covered it with his arms, hoping she wouldn't notice his sobs. She had already withdrawn from him, from the situation, and was looking away, out the window, into the darkness. The life they created had ended without permission, cut off before growth had taken hold, maturity became reality, promise happened. He picked up the telephone and punched out the priest's number. Their suitcases still sat in the driveway.

☙   ☙   ☙

We mourn the loss of promise, the unfulfilled, the unrealized. We mourn a reality that marks our lives. How can life lose meaning even before it has had a chance to happen?

How? When we allow life to die—figuratively, symbolically, actually—before it has had a chance to live, it is because we do not dare give it that chance for life. The death of a young person calls all that forth in us. The young life that did not have a chance to live confronts each of us with a stark reality: the dead life is the very one that we have denied.

We are not sure what that means, but one thing we know: anything is preferable to facing that reality, and it is the reality that death is the absence of growth. The challenge this death offers is pain. Such pain is a double-edged sword that requires leaving the known and entering the unknown. Neither is welcome, even though we know that growth only occurs in letting go of the safe, the known, the familiar—and reaching out for the new and unknown. Not to let go is to assure death, yet we are told from our earliest years...

...look before you leap...

...never quit a job until you have a new one...

...the way to get in to Harvard is...

...success is assured if you marry the right person...

...better safe than sorry...

...you'll never regret going to law school...

...a bird in the hand is worth two in the bush.

42

After Moses led his people out of the bondage of slavery in Egypt into the freedom of new life in the wilderness, they came close to rebellion and in their great fear they cried to the Lord and said to Moses, "Is it because there are no graves in Egypt that you have taken us away to die in the wilderness? What have you done to us in bringing us out of Egypt? Is not this what we said to you in Egypt, 'Let us alone and let us serve the Egyptians'? For it would be better to serve the Egyptians than to die in the wilderness."

Yet into the wilderness we must travel, as we grow, if we would grow.

     ❧   ❧   ❧

There is a scene at the conclusion of *Winnie the Pooh* which marks the end of Christopher Robin's childhood. His world has changed. One age is about to end and a new age to begin.

> ...Then, suddenly again, Christopher Robin, who was still looking at the world, with his chin in his hands, called out "Pooh!"
>
> "Yes?" said Pooh.
>
> "When I'm - when - Pooh!"
>
> "Yes, Christopher Robin?"
>
> "I'm not going to do Nothing any more."
>
> "Never again?"
>
> "Well, not so much. They don't let you."
>
> Pooh waited for him to go on, but he was silent again.
>
> "Yes, Christopher Robin?" said Pooh helpfully.
>
> "Pooh, when I'm—you know—when I'm not doing Nothing, will you come up here sometimes?"
>
> "Just Me?"
>
> "Yes, Pooh."
>
> "Will you be here too?"

"Yes, Pooh, I will be, really. I promise I will be, Pooh."

"That's good," said Pooh.

Pooh thought for a while.

"How old shall I be then?"

"Ninety-nine."

Pooh nodded.

"I promise." he said

Still with his eyes on the world, Christopher Robin put out a hand and felt for Pooh's paw.

"Pooh," said Christopher Robin earnestly, "if I—if I'm not quite—" he stopped and tried again—

"Pooh, whatever happens, you will understand, won't you?"

"Understand what?"

"Oh, nothing." He laughed and jumped to his feet.

"Come on!"

"Where?" said Pooh.

"Anywhere," said Christopher Robin.

The possibilities for death are endless if we wish to remain in the slavery of Egypt. To enter the wilderness and to allow new life to happen means leaving behind what has been familiar, comforting, nourishing, but if we do not, then death is certain. On the other hand, to lay claim to the eternal life offered to us by God in Christ brings the possibility of new life that is unlimited. The alternative is death at an early age. The choice is always ours.

ㅤㅤㅤ❧ㅤㅤㅤ❧ㅤㅤㅤ❧

After we pray for the dead, we pray for those who mourn.

Most merciful God, whose wisdom is beyond our understanding, deal graciously with NN. in their grief. Surround

44

*them with your love, that they may not be overwhelmed by
their loss, but have confidence in your goodness, and strength
to meet the days to come; through Jesus Christ our Lord.
Amen.*

Grief is the process by which God transforms loss into
new life. Grief is frequent and comes to each of us. When
we turn from it, we die before our time. We are best
served, therefore, when we do not turn away, but this requires the strength and support that comes through our
prayer for those who grieve. This collect is a focus for
that opportunity.

When we witness loss, any loss, we own it, and when
we own it, we share it. This moment, as we watch over
those who mourn, for whom we care, our prayer surrounds them and empowers them to be uplifted by the
love of God.

Grief is overpowering. Loss removes perspective.
Whatever the occasion—death, departure, accident, even
a computer error that destroys fifty never-to-be-re-
covered pages when it happens, there is only emptiness, pure vacuum, no feeling. Whatever is said or done,
it just doesn't matter. Past, present, future, they all
vanish. Time numbs pain, but that pain does not vanish.
It seeks a new level, where hurt is replaced by healing
and the renewed awareness that the world is defined by
God's love.

᪥   ᪥   ᪥

John Cheever's first published short story, written at
the age of seventeen, describes his expulsion from Thayer
Academy in Massachusetts in the eleventh grade.

It didn't come all at once. It took a very long time. First I had a skirmish with the English department and then with all the other departments. Pretty soon something had to be done....

The spring of five months ago was the most beautiful spring I have ever lived in. The year before I had not known all about the trees and the heavy peach blossoms and the tea-colored brooks that shook down over the brown rocks. Five months ago it was spring, and I was in school....

In the spring I was glad to leave school. Everything outside was elegant and savage and fleshy. Everything inside was slow and cool and vacant. It seemed a shame to stay inside.

But in a little while the spring went. I was left outside and there was no spring. I did not want to go in again. I would not have gone in again for anything. I was sorry, but I was not sorry over the fact I had gone out. I was sorry that the outside and the inside could not have been open to one another. I was sorry that there were roofs on the classrooms and trousers on the legs of the instructors to insulate their contacts. I was not sorry that I had left school. I was sorry that I left for the reasons I left...

And now it is August. The orchards are stinking ripe. The tea-colored brooks run beneath the rocks. There is sediment on the stone and no wind in the willows. Everyone is preparing to go back to school. I have no school to go back to.

Was Cheever renewed through this adolescent death? There is no guarantee for any of us, none, save the fact that we may be certain that we will have loss and grief. The possibility of renewal always waits, but it is never assured.

&a.   &a.   &a.

...Late on a Friday afternoon his boss entered the office casually and without warning. The conversation began quietly, too quietly. His trivial "agenda" was merely a cover.

"There is another reason for this visit," his boss finally said, and as soon as the words were out, the man knew what was next. Then numbness spread throughout his body, preventing feeling and response. Everything that existed before had just ended. He was being fired.

"There is something we have to talk about. It isn't easy, but I've thought about it for a long time, and I've talked with those who know and love you best. There is no other way. It's time, time for a change."

"What kind of change?"

"You've been here long enough. I mean...don't get me wrong. What has been has been good, very good. You've done a great job. But you're just not the person we need in the job right now. Times have changed. Nothing is the same as the day you started. The world is a different place. There are different demands, and they call for different responses. You are a fine and wonderful person, and I shall always love and respect you, but you just aren't the right person any more. It doesn't work. You don't work. It's time for a change."

He tried desperately to speak. He could not. It was as if he had been hypnotized. When the conversation finally ended, he realized that it had lasted an hour. Time had no meaning. It had not even stood still. It had never been. Still numb, he moved in a daze, not knowing where or why. He wanted to cry. And then it was all over, as quickly as it had begun, concluded in a haze with a final exchange and a handshake—of all things. He stood alone, wondering where or how he stood, before the

47

spasms rose from the depths of his being to wrack him. Then tears.

Sitting down into a chair in the corner of the office, he allowed the feelings of loss to sweep over him. Once there had been something, but now, where that something had once been, there was nothing. Often he had wondered what complete absence felt like. Now he knew. He could finally believe in nothingness. It surrounded him.

For some time his feet refused to take him anywhere at all. He continued to sit motionless and alone until, face streaked, eyes glazed, he said aloud, "What's to be done?" Unsure to whom he spoke, he rose, and went to wash his face and ready himself for home. The car, where was the car? Down, down into the cavern below, the struggle to remember where to turn in a world gone awry, robbed of its reality and reliability. He found the car and then the exit and the expressway. Public Radio, "All Things Considered," the familiar voices of Noah Adams and Susan Stamberg reassured him.

Home at last, he followed his feet to her. He found her kneeling, hard at work, in the farthest corner of the attic cleaning up the accumulation of many years. He told her. Words between them were halting, garbled, and finally, unnecessary. Communication at the time of death is of a different order, sustained by a look, an embrace, hours and years of shared history, common knowledge of the good, the bad, the indifferent.

The love they had for one another did not stand alone. Soon a telephone call brought two good friends, and then their numbers included family, all the family, summoned, gathered to bear the death together. Tears, sorrow and loss remained, but the immediate world had increased in size and depth to embrace the hurt, and slowly, ever so slowly, to heal the pain.

                            ea.   ea.   ea.

Christ comes in many ways. Through the love of family and friends, their prayers and presence, the offering of themselves, their efforts to place their love over and around the hurt. The hurt is ours alone, but they experience it too.

He comes through the assurance of his own death and resurrection and the conviction that death recurs and death remains. There is no possible way to live life without loss, but loss never means the end of love. Through Christ loss announces the possibility of new life, new birth, new hope. The ashes, the sorrow, the memory remain, but through it and from it, there is more.

CHAPTER III

Raised in Power

The Liturgy of the Word

H IS SENSE OF HER nearness and the possibility of her disapproval of this moment made him uneasy. He shifted in his seat. Could Nancy be here? "Cut it out!" he said to himself, and then almost out loud, "She's dead." A voice sounded in his ear that said, "Am I?" He turned around, but all he saw were faces, a mass of faces, some known, some unknown. One or two smiled, others looked away. He turned forward and brought his head to rest on the front of the pew before him, covered it with both arms, and carefully emptied his mind, slowly, systematically, until he could see and hear only Nancy.

Nancy—when they first met. Nancy—when they married. Nancy—lying in the hospital bed, holding Anne, newly born. Nancy—sleeping next to him. Nancy—walking through the kitchen door at the end of the day. Nancy—sitting at the other end of the dining room table on Christmas Day. Nancy calling to him, "Come and have breakfast." His body shook, "I love you," he whispered. No answer.

He was overwhelmed by loneliness. These past three terrible days a new pattern had begun. Living alone, surrounded on every side by the marks of her presence and vitality, he kept hearing her voice, "Come and have breakfast," her step. He waited in bed at night for her breathing. What got to him was the way nothing ever changed in the house. The way he left it in the morning was the way it remained when he returned in the dark of evening. He kept expecting the phone to ring. This time, surely, it would be Nancy. Coming down the stairs and turning into the living room, he would see her sitting next to the fireplace in the wing chair, reading. He would notice that her bathrobe was not hanging on the bathroom door, and for one split second thought she was showering in the children's bathroom.

Each time, mercifully, he sat down and cried and cried. Let it all go. Then he would force himself to stand and walk through the entire house, check every single photograph, particularly the two of them standing together on a sunny afternoon, harassed, just married, but still smiling, surrounded by parents, relatives, children. It did not seem so long ago.

But now, sitting here in this pew, it was worse. He felt trapped, caught, helpless, useless, and so alone. He opened his eyes. Was she there? Standing in front of him—Nancy! No, not Nancy, but his daughter who looked so much like her. Anne, no longer a new born baby snuggled in her mother's arms, but a grown woman, stood directly before him, at the lectern. She began the first reading, from the book of the prophet Isaiah.

THE OLD TESTAMENT LESSON

*The Spirit of the Lord God
is upon me,
because the Lord has annointed me
to bring glad tidings to the afflicted;
he has sent me to bind up the
brokenhearted,
to proclaim liberty to the captive,
and the opening of the prison
to those who are bound;
to proclaim the year of the Lord's
favor,
and the day of vengence of our God;
to comfort all who mourn,
to grant to those who mourn in Zion—
to give them a garland instead of a
faint spirit;
that they may be called oaks of
righteousness,
the planting of the Lord, that
he may be glorified.*

ISAIAH 61:1-3

The Liturgy of the Word contains three lessons and a psalm, each containing an interpretation of death They are a strong testimony from the community of faith, which creates a framework and an opportunity for us to see more clearly and with greater perspective that death occurs in a context created by God.

The Old Testament lesson from Isaiah describes a time of exile—separation and captivity—a time when the familiar has been replaced by the foreign, the comfortable by the comfortless, but even here God is present, even in captivity.

Captivity is experienced loss. Value—either the life of another or the value of our very own life—has been taken from us. We were not consulted. Now we are brokenhearted, afflicted, deprived of joy. Seemingly forever lost, prison binds us, darkness blinds us, we are held captive in an unknown land, bereft of familiar faces or landmarks. All we have are our memories. At such a time as this we are diminished, paralyzed, unable to move and act, even to speak.

Conrad, the central figure in Judith Guest's novel, *Ordinary People*, caught in the grip of depression and crippling guilt after the accidental death of his older brother, lies in bed in the early morning. He has no reason to get up. "To have a reason to get up in the morning, it is necessary to possess…a belief of some kind.…He rolls onto his stomach, pulling the pillow tight around his head, blocking out the sharp arrows of sun that pierce through the window."

Death means the loss not only of a person whom we love, or the job of a lifetime, or health or memory or marriage. Death may be all of these, but it is also much more. When death happens, it appears that we have lost everything: our bearings, our sense of self and place and value and faith. What is left is nothing, and it feels as though we are in prison. It is a prison not of our own making, nor of God's, nor indeed of anyone we can name or see. Only the prison is very real and very lonely, and there are no doors or windows or keepers or keys.

To know loss is to be held captive.

֍   ֍   ֍

...Depression began for him at mid-life, the final and total loss of the older generation, full responsibiity for his family and all of his own actions. Worst of all, he realized that for him professional advancement had ended. He was at the end of the road—caught in his job, caught in his house, caught in his marriage. Caught. The spirit drained from him daily, weekly, monthly. His employer placed him on medical leave.

"Each day was much like the one before and after it," he told me. "My wife left for her job at eight. She had long since ceased to try to get me out of bed. It was impossible. No reason. I lay there and lay there and lay there, oblivious to time, surrounded by the complete absence of purpose. Finally, perhaps by ten o'clock—but I really don't know; there was no sense of time—with the greatest of effort, I would roll from the bed and onto the floor, and lay there for perhaps an hour. Gradually, bit by bit, I would crawl to the bathroom.

"The rest of the day went by in this same laborious, tedious fashion. Every movement was agony, undertaken only because I knew that paralysis would signal my own death. The day was endless, and it was also momentary, but by the time she returned at five, I might have been able to get to the landing on the stairs. She would open the front door, walk into the house, turn and come up the stairs to find me crouched there, huddled in the corner, just where those stairs," he pointed, "turn toward the front hall."

֍   ֍   ֍

Isaiah wrote at a time when the longest winter of the soul for his people, what seemed like a never-ending period of captivity, was bursting open into a new kind of opportunity. Isaiah's words are not for his age only, but for all ages. Jesus quoted these words as he announced the beginning of his ministry. We are all familiar with death and loss and captivity. What we need to know is that they issue in new life.

For those who mourn, those lost and alone, Isaiah proclaims comfort, symbolized by flowers, the presence of color and life and scent rather than the absence of hope. The sound of praise replaces silence. Those who have been bound will be released. The Lord, the essence of life, fills life with hope. Where once there was only loss, freedom follows captivity.

æ   æ   æ

...After the telephone call, he retreated into depression. All color and life left his face. Nothing seemed to matter, neither the routine nor the unusual. Life flattened out, devoid of peaks and valleys; all was gray and bland.

The children tried first and then his minister. Doctors expressed concern, and elderly family members worried and fussed at him. He paid little attention, and allowed himself to be carried along by the ongoing patterns of daily life that surrounded him, acting more like an old-fashioned wind-up toy than the purposeful man he had always been.

Quite without warning she appeared, his wife's childhood friend who had disappeared into the mists of the Christmas card list. Long ago she and her husband had moved to a distant city, and they had lost real touch with

one another. But she heard, and when she heard, she
came. She came because she knew. Her husband had
died of cancer last February, and she knew about loss
and loneliness.

THE PSALM

Lord, you have searched me out and known me;
  you know my sitting down and my rising up;
  you discern my thoughts from afar.

You trace my journeys and my resting-places
  and you are aquainted with all my ways.

Indeed, there is not a word on my lips,
  but you, O Lord, know it altogether.

You press upon me behind and before
  and lay your hand upon me.

Such knowledge is too wonderful for me:
  it is so high that I cannot attain to it.

Where can I go then from your Spirit?
  where can I flee from your presence?

If I climb up to heaven, you are there;
  if I make the grave my bed, you are there also.

If I take the wings of the morning
  and dwell in the uttermost parts of the sea,

Even there your hand will lead me
  and your right hand hold me fast.

If I say, "Surely the darkness will cover me,
  and the light around me turn to night,"

Darkness is not dark to you;
the night is as bright as the day;
  darkness and light to you are both alike.

PSALM 139:1-11

In this psalm, more than in any other passage in the Bible, it is made abundantly clear that God is involved in the totality of our lives. There is nothing we do or say or think that God does not know, even before it happens. No place, no person, no event enters our lives without his knowledge. This is hardly a guarantee of happiness for ever after, but it does mean that we are never alone, no matter how weak or vulnerable or little or lonely or lost.

ﷺ   ﷺ   ﷺ

"I couldn't stay in my wife's room for more than ten minutes at a time. Walking back and forth in the hospital corridor let me know I was alive. I felt her pleading with me to go with her, and I pulled back from what seemed like a death grip.

"Marriage is not forever, only until we are parted by death. That was about to happen, any day, only she wouldn't let go. She hung on and hung on, tenacious lover to the very end. What about beyond the end?

Would she be pulling, calling from the grave? Would we ever really be parted?

"Returning to her room from the corridor, I reached down and grasped the hand that hung limp and lifeless beside the mattress. She opened her eyes, tried to smile and say, 'I love you.' The lips formed the words, but there was no sound. Her beauty had long since gone, skin drawn and lifeless, lips parched, eyes clouded, hair disheveled, but I loved her more than ever before. More. Sexual attraction had been transformed. Where it had once been, now there was a bond more powerful even than furious bone-to-bone passion.

"Her eyes closed, and as I looked down on her face, now barely alive, I realized that soon I would never see it again. She was sleeping, and so I cried, 'I love you, God, how I love you.'"

      ❧   ❧   ❧

At the time of death we are laid bare. Nothing can be hidden, either from ourselves or from God.

      ❧   ❧   ❧

…We gathered once a week, the first thing in the morning, to pray together the daily office. The discipline, the opportunity, the presence of God brought us nearer one another, able to speak and pray of loss and hope, of discerning God's will.

"When is it that God makes himself known?" asked the young man sitting in the bright sun at the conclusion of the office on an autumn morning.

"Always," she replied, from across the room. "Always, if we listen and wait. God is always at work in each of our lives. God is always making himself known. Only we don't allow ourselves to hear."

She spoke with urgency. "Ken and I were married for twenty-eight years. One day I took him to the airport, and I watched him walk through those big double doors, away from me, to catch his plane, and I never saw him again. Never. The next morning he was dead, fifty years old, and I was alone, with nothing.

"It was then that I finally said, 'God. You're all I've got. There's nothing else.' That was when I started to listen. That was when I started to hear."

She stopped speaking, and we all listened in the silence. It is the time when we take time to listen to the only One who might have something to say.

ਨੇ   ਨੇ   ਨੇ

> I sought the Lord, and afterward I knew
> He moved my soul to seek him, seeking me;
> It was not I that found, O Saviour true;
> No, I was found of Thee.

Sooner or later, it all goes. Each of us is left to make the longest journey alone. Every support, known or unknown, remembered or forgotten, is removed. Loss is the pervasive and prevailing fact of human existence, and at that moment, more than at any other, we are searched and known and found.

ਨੇ   ਨੇ   ਨੇ

...For forty years he had worked faithfully and well and risen through the ranks, achieved prominence and exercised leadership, made his mark. The day came for retirement, the dinner, the speeches and the watch. His wife already dead, he moved away to live alone.

Six months passed. No one saw him until he reappeared to attend the funeral of an older and retired colleague. This colleague despised church, especially funerals, but he and his wife had agreed that when his time came, it would be a church funeral, as long as those present could share a pleasant social hour following the service, with plenty of time for give and take.

People milled around, shaking hands, exchanging pleasantries, remembering this and that about Howard. The two men met at the very center, one the older, recently retired mentor, and the other his younger aquaintance, follower, and admirer.

The older spoke directly, forcefully. "It has been on my mind to write you and thank you for your very kind letter to me when I retired."

"There was no reason for you to write. It was my privilege to write to you and thank you for all you have meant to me all these years."

"No, no. I should have written," the older man replied.

It was the only letter he had received.

◦ ◦ ◦

That person speaks to us as God. Loss is the prevailing and pervasive fact of human existence, but even in the midst of loss, especially in the midst of loss, God is present. Finally, there is no other source of help, none at all, save God.

THE NEW TESTAMENT LESSON

But in fact Christ has been raised from the dead, the first fruits of those who have fallen asleep . For as by a man came death, by a man has come also the resurrection of the dead. For as in Adam all die, so also in Christ shall all be made alive. But each in his own order: Christ the first fruits, then at his coming those who belong to Christ. Then comes the end, when he delivers the kingdom to God the Father after destroying every rule and every authority and power. For he must reign until he has put all his enemies under his feet. The last enemy to be destroyed is death....

But someone will ask, "How are the dead raised? With what kind of body do they come?" You foolish man! What you sow does not come to life unless it dies. And what you sow is not the body which is to be, but a bare kernel, perhaps of wheat or of some other grain. But God gives it a body as he has chosen and to each kind of seed its own body....

So it is with the resurrection of the dead. What is sown is perishable, what is raised is imperishable. It is sown in dishonor, it is raised in glory. It is sown in weakness, it is raised in power. It is sown a physical body, it is raised a spiritual body. If there is a physical body, there is also a spiritual body.

For this perishable nature must put on the imperishable, and this mortal nature must put on immortality. When the perishable puts on the imperishable, and the mortal puts on immortality, then shall come to pass the saying that is written:

"Death is swallowed up in victory.
O death, where is thy victory?
O death, where is thy sting?"

The sting of death is sin, and the power of sin is the law. But thanks be to God, who gives us the victory through our Lord Jesus Christ.

1 CORINTHIANS 15: 20-26, 35-38, 42-44, 53-57

This is the earliest and most important testimony to the resurrection and its place in the Christian faith. Paul proclaims that there is new life—resurrection—in Christ. Life as we have known it ends. It does not go on forever, but at the very same time, death also is not the end. Death is the passage through which we travel to the victory of new life through Christ.

"How are the dead raised? With what kind of body do they come?" These are the right questions for a culture that tells us we are what we eat, that judges us by every aspect of our appearance. We are led to believe that what encloses and surrounds us—automobiles, clothes, houses—also defines us. Who we are is how we appear. We are our body, that outward appearance which presents our inner being to the world.

ᕫ   ᕫ   ᕫ

...Her grandmother bought a special hat to be buried in. "They never do your hair right when you're dead," she explained.

The hat was made of straw, the brim covered with silk flowers that had curled and changed color with age.

When the day came, after her hair had been fixed by the undertaker, the young woman put the hat on her grandmother's head, and stood back to admire it, uncertain whether grandmother would be pleased. The funeral home had insisted on visiting hours, and they seemed a good idea, especially when one after another of grandmother's friends commented on how well she looked. "Just like herself, dear Frances. The hat is perfect!"

&a.   &a.   &a.

What the woman looked like in her coffin was an approximation, an image, a reminder to family and friends, of what Frances looked like the day she died. Somehow we deceive ourselves into believing this is important, and we go to great and even ridiculous ends so to clothe or surround ourselves with things that we look good—better and better—although not at all like our inner self. St. Paul expands this reality into a new dimension and tells us, "What you sow does not come to life unless it dies."

Resurrection promises a new self. The photograph of the child contains the promise of an adult face, but what we see in the frame is a child, not an adult. The person once known by a nickname, "little Billy," lives no more. The stages of growth and development have brought changes, the end of one kind of person and the birth of someone new. The marriage of forty years is no longer fueled by the same hot passion shared at age twenty, but there is a new bond that is deeper, stronger, mellower. The abiding truths we learned in kindergarten were appropriate when we were five years old. Those truths remain, but later they assume new and different forms of

expression. We may long to gather again in a circle on the
rug with our teacher, or hold hands with a best friend on
the way to the cafeteria or on the bus going home, but
that is no longer how we express ourselves in such a situation. Then we find new ways to be in touch and to be
alive. "So it is with the resurrection of the dead."

         ❦   ❦   ❦

...At the service for a lapsed Roman Catholic at the
funeral home, the minister was asked to read a passage
from *Walden Pond*—"about a worm," he remarked that
evening. "It was all about a worm hatching into a butterfly, or a moth. God, it depressed me."

"Why? Isn't it meant to be a promise of something better?"

"Not for this poor old unknown guy who spent his life
thinking only of sex and money and booze. He's dead.
Who cares? Least of all him. So I'm called in to bless his
death and make it holy, since no one else gives a damn.
Then I'm told that I cannot read what I want to read, but
have to read something from Henry David Thoreau, who
knew the deceased about as well as he knew Jesus. That's
depressing."

"So, what would you prefer? That they carry the body
from the morgue to the crematorium with no ceremony?"

"What's ceremony, if no one's present who knew him
or loved him or had the slightest idea of what might be
next—for him or me or you or anyone else, for that matter."

"You miss the point. It only matters if one person, one
person alone was there."

"Who?"

"Jesus. It was Jesus who died for him and made new life possible."

❧ ❧ ❧

...Long before her death, she would sit with me in the evening and ask me what she would look like when she died. I read to her from the letter St. Paul wrote to the Corinthians about seeds and resurrection bodies. She looked disgusted. "Wheat," she said disdainfully. "Wheat!"

"No, no, no, Grandmother. Don't be so literal. Wheat is a metaphor. It doesn't mean that you are wheat, but the body you are sitting in is like a seed, a kernel. After you are dead and buried, the resurrection will be new life growing from who you have been and are now, just as the stalk grows out of the seed. You will be different, like the tulip from a bulb, the butterfly from the cocoon, the frog from the tadpole. Even like a person who grows from the union of sperm and egg. It makes perfect sense. Listen."

Once more I read aloud, as she sat by the fire, covered with her afghan, wide awake, trying to visualize what it would be like when her life was over. I finished the passage.

"So who made him so smart? Does he think he knows all the answers?"

"Maybe. How do I know? But I've always thought he was someone a lot like you, someone who woke up each morning to a day he must somehow live, to a self he must somehow be, to a mystery he could not fathom, if only the mystery of life."

"He could have left it right there and cut out the talk about wheat."

"Only he didn't, and he couldn't. What he thought and wrote and told people has been handed down. It could be, like you said, that he thought too much, or maybe he really did have a bright idea, the right idea, and that bright idea says it all."

We sat in silence. Something was going on that was unreal. Here I was, a young woman, trying to explain to my wise old grandmother, whom I loved more than anyone I had ever known, what was going to happen to her! It was terribly important. Whatever was going to happen would happen, in spite of my words, but somehow, I wanted her to understand, now, what I knew to be true.

Then it came to me.

"Grandmother. Listen to me. One last time. The reason we are having this conversation is because you wonder what is going to happen when you die. I love you. I have always loved you and will always love you. My love will not let go. But my love is nothing compared to God's love. His love brought you into being and holds you tight forever and ever. His love will continue to hold you after you are dead, and your old body has been buried. Only then God will hold your new body in a new way. That new way is resurrection and resurrection will be different, as different from who you are now as you are different from a seed or cocoon or sperm and egg."

THE GOSPEL

The Liturgy of the Word brings the insights of Holy Scripture to this particular moment and marking of a death. The entire service, the Burial of the Dead, has been placed in this context by the opening anthems, each an essential scriptural assertion. As the liturgy proceeds, we move through the opening collects to ever-deeper biblical proclamation. From the Old Testament, we first hear Isaiah speak of God's presence and participation in the pain and promise of Babylonian captivity, and then we hear the Psalmist make very clear that God is always present in everything we do and wherever we find ourselves. The Epistle places us squarely in the midst of St. Paul's powerful explanation of what resurrection means when actually experienced, and now Paul's understanding is underscored and undergirded with the Gospel. Only one of the four gospels is read, but each reading is a passage from John, and each affirms in Jesus' own words his presence with us in the eternal life we share.

Martha said to Jesus, "Lord, if you had been here, my brother would not have died. And even now I know that whatever you ask from God, God will give you." Jesus said to her, "Your brother will rise again." Martha said to him, "I know that he will rise again in the resurrection at the last day." Jesus said to her. "I am the resurrection and the life; he who believes in me, though he die, yet shall he live, and whoever lives and believes in me shall never die. Do you believe this? She said to him, "Yes, Lord; I believe that you are the Christ, the Son of God, he who is coming into the world."

JOHN 11: 21-27

...On his seventh birthday, his father gave him a small, red one-horsepower outboard motor. One cylinder, a foretaste of the consumer glut to come after the war, this little "putt-putt" was a rarity, and the boy's pride and joy. At a barely perceptible speed, he could go anywhere on the lake.

And he did, until one Saturday afternoon in mid-summer, returning home across a broad and deep part of the lake, there was an unaccustomed clanking noise, the sound of flying metal within the engine, and then silence. He wrapped and rewrapped the starter cord and pulled and pulled and pulled. Nothing. Finally, he got out the oars and rowed.

After he tied up at the dock, carefully removed the motor, placed it in the wheelbarrow and pushed it up to the maintenance shed, he found Mr. Williamson, who just happened to be there before stopping work for supper.

Mr. Williamson was the most important person in his life. The family camp that had brought them together was staffed entirely by college and graduate students. Mr. Williamson, who was in charge of all outside operations, was a doctoral candidate in clinical psychology, a man of great wisdom and skill, who knew everything, or so it seemed. He had grown up on a scrub farm in central Texas, drove a truck, smoked a pipe, answered endless questions, and offered wisdom to this seven-year-old.

"Mr Williamson. Something terrible has happened to my putt-putt." He explained the symptoms. "Will you please fix it? I know you can. Please fix it!"

Nothing happened quickly in the first year of World War II, and it took the rest of the summer and careful reading of the manual and sending for parts, but as the summer ended, boy and man took one last ride in the boat with the small outboard motor that Mr. Williamson had repaired.

Thirty years later, Mr. and Mrs. Williamson came for a weekend visit. As they sat down for dinner and said grace, it brought to mind the earlier time. Did Mr. Williamson remember the summer of the one-horsepower outboard motor?

"Do I remember! Of course I remember. Why do I remember? I'll tell you why. To this day I know nothing, absolutely nothing about gasoline motors. When my lawn mower stops, I take it down to the shop on the corner to have it repaired. But when you brought that outboard to me and asked me to fix it, you believed in all your heart that I could, and, right then, I knew I could too because you believed in me."

&ea.   &ea.   &ea.

"He who believes in me, though he die, yet shall he live." Resurrection is powered by belief. The power of God only breaks through and into our lives when we are open and allow that to happen. The channel of that openness is belief.

Beyond belief, there is something else. It is that resurrection is possible only when there is the willingness to let go of the past and move into a different kind of future.

&ea.   &ea.   &ea.

...The cancer began in her left ear. After the diagnosis she could recall the occasional earaches, but at the beginning they had been so infrequent that she had given them no real thought. Much later, now well past the age of thirty, when the earaches became daily, incessant, excruciating, and weeping blood, she went for help. Help was a tall man in a white coat, poking and peering into her ear, using a round mirror with a hole in its center.

Just before she left the doctor's office on that day of discovery, the doctor took x-rays that brought back memories of days in the dentist's chair as a little girl and the impossible attempts to make her teeth straight. They had always been crooked even after all that. All for nothing. Now, as she rose to leave the doctor's office, he told her he'd need some time to think about what he'd found. He'd be in touch.

Several days later the telephone rang, and he asked if she could come by that afternoon on her way home. When she arrived, no one was in the waiting room. Even the receptionist had gone home. When he came to the door, she noticed that he looked a little different, while still in the white coat and round mirror. He asked her to sit down. There was a long pause before he began to speak. She knew that the news could not be good.

She heard little of what he said. She knew it was bad. Cancer, well spread. There was little hope. Still, if she were willing, he would recommend surgery, massive facial surgery to remove all that was already diseased, and then go deeper, much deeper. She would lose at least half of the lower jaw, most of her right cheek bone, some skull. Her face would be changed forever. It would not be her own. Later perhaps—but only perhaps—they could rebuild her face using bone from the hip. The outcome was an open question.

But she agreed. What else was there to do?

She drove home in a daze, and remained that way for several days until she awoke in the recovery room, covered with bandages, unable to see or feel. Life as she

71

had known it had been removed from her, and she was surrounded only by distance that separated her from everything and everyone she had known, including her husband. As it turned out, especially her husband—who afterward would tell her that she was no longer the woman he had married, and he wanted another.

The surgery had been quick, but the death of what had been was long and agonizing. Loss, change, alcohol, more loss, more change, and then recovery. Not rebirth, yet. Was she the same person she had once been? It didn't really matter. What was important was that she was a new person, a person whose face barely resembled the one she had once worn. What was important was to face it, her face, and with that face to reenter the world. She found support through new friends, friends who had also suffered great loss and change, who needed strength and support to face a new life. Everyone has to, but it's easier when you are not alone.

Her new life, however, was far more than an activity to help herself by helping others, although this was how she spent her days. Her new life meant that she became a new person, consistent with who she had always been, but more. She was a person who had been brought through death, given eyes to see and the heart to grasp a whole new life. Now she offered others this same gift. Life had a new dimension.

The cosmetologist she finally consulted said to her, "If you let me, I can make you beautiful."

"But I am beautiful," was her reply.

"Let not your hearts be troubled; believe in God, believe also in me. In my Father's house are many rooms; if it were not so, would I have told you that I go to prepare a place for you? And

when I go and prepare a place for you, I will come again and will take you to myself, that where I am you may be also. And you know the way where I am going." Thomas said to him, "Lord, we do not know where you are going; how can we know the way?" Jesus said to him, "I am the way, and the truth, and the life; no one comes to the Father, but by me."

JOHN 14:1-6

Many persons grew up hearing, again and again, the familiar saying offered by mother or Aunt Jennie or the grandmother who always smelled of lavender water and whom we loved more than life itself: "When God closes one door, he always opens another." No doubt we thought, "Oh, there she goes again, the dear old Pollyanna." Little did we know that those words were a close paraphrase of this gospel.

&.   &.   &.

Jane entered her husband's hospital room just as the doctor was completing his examination. He suggested that they step into the corridor.

"Jim's heart has not suffered any real damage," he told her, "but he's still pretty sick and he'll need a lot of rest and rehabilitative therapy. If that happens, he'll recover fully and live several more years."

Jane burst into tears. "Oh Henry, thank you, thank you! That's wonderful. We were all so afraid that Jim was gone, and I just couldn't face that, not yet, not now."

"There is one other thing that you should know," the doctor added. "Jim will have to give up all smoking and drinking, immediately and permanently. Not even one

73

drink and not a single cigarette. Now, let's both go back into the room and talk with him."

The two moved back from the corridor into Jim's room to find that in the few minutes they had been gone, he had died. Minutes earlier, he had been fine.

Years later, when these moments were history, Jane would say with a smile, "Jim must have heard Henry telling me the news about drinking and smoking, and he decided, then and there, that life just wasn't worth it, not without booze and cigarettes."

ૐ   ૐ   ૐ

New life may not always be welcome, and we may reject it. The new room God has for us to enter may hold no interest or appeal. There are, however, other more powerful times when, painful as it is to close one door that represents the better part of life, we are drawn, inexorably, into that new room, and we never go alone.

ૐ   ૐ   ૐ

...On a Monday evening in mid-May, returning from an evening of food and company, two old friends lingered, parked in the driveway to allow time for saying goodbye. One of them started to get out, then stopped. "You should be one of the first to know that our marriage is over. We've tried and tried. It's just no good. Not any more, if it ever was. Sally and I, we're through." But before he left his friend, the two men agreed to at least one last long conversation.

So it was that during the following summer he and his wife visited for what all of them suspected might be the last time. The four friends spent many hours talking about the past, probing its reality, trying to discover what hope there might be for the future. The conversation between the two whose marriage had ended often became bitter. Harsh words were exchanged between husband and wife, words marked by terrible honesty. From time to time, there were expressions of tenderness and moments of hope, but it was clear that the marriage was over. Death had occurred. It was too late.

A year passed, and the time came for another visit. This time he came alone, already divorced, accompanied only by his children. It was a lonely and reflective time; this place was for him still full of the painful memories of the insults shouted, wounds received and delivered. He seemed vague, only occasionally speaking of what was really on his mind—the new woman, whom he would creep away to telephone. As his visit came to an end, he finally spoke of his new-found infatuation. He was once again, no, he corrected himself, for the very first time, learning to love. It was all very new and scary. How could anyone—especially her, who had come to know him so very well—love a man like him?

Another year. Another visit. Now they were a couple, engaged to be married. A new bond had been formed. What once was dead had been born a second time.

THE HOMILY

The homily is not a eulogy. To deliver a eulogy is a pre-Christian custom which honors a complete life that has now completely ended, but even as the life ends, the eulogy keeps it alive, saying such things as: "The world will not long remember anything we say here, but no one will ever, ever forget what Sam did for you and me and countless hundreds of others." For the person who has left a job after long service and understood the harsh reality of the old saying, "When you're out, you're out," such eulogistic words may be kind and even well intentioned, but they are not true.

The eulogy praises a life that has ended, understanding it as the single-handed accomplishment of the one who has died. The Christian, on the other hand, understands death as an ending that marks a new beginning and an accomplishment of the work of God through Christ.

Death in the context of the Burial of the Dead is concerned neither with immortality nor our accomplishments. These belong only to God, not to human beings. A belief in immortality is the hope that life never ends. One way or another, immortality asserts that death does not really happen. Death is merely a horizon, the limit of our sight, and there are countless ways to extend our vision and our reach.

The hope of immortality creates life insurance, a contract encouraging the purchaser to believe that it will guarantee the continuation of certain convictions and the direct benefit of others in the name and memory of the deceased. The goal of life insurance is a good and kind act whose motivation is immortality.

The "living will" is a document that declares the donor's desire not to have life unduly and articifially continued through medical life-support systems. The document also provides for the donation of vital organs for the use of others who are still living and in need of a kidney or a liver or a set of eyes. On the one hand the "living will" acknowledges clearly the inevitability of death, but on the other hand it is driven by the hope that at least some parts of my body will continue to live, even after I am dead. The living will a is noble, kind, and good idea whose motivation is immortality.

The "planned gift" is the gift that goes on giving long after the donor has died. While the planned gift comes in many forms, the most common form is made during the lifetime of the donor to a charitable institution, a gift that assures a certain annual income during that person's life-time. At the time of death, however, the property desig-nated by the planned gift passes to the charitable institution, and its benefits will become permanent. The planned gift is a thoughtful and generous statement whose motivation is immortality.

Over against immortality and the pride of human ac-complishment, the homily places death, especially this particular death, in the context of the Christian gospel. It is not we who live but Christ who lives through us, and as this person's life in Christ has now ended, so too another life in Christ may now begin.

ᵛ   ᵛ   ᵛ

...The marriage was still young and bore the promise of remaining as alive in the future as in its very first days. The three small children were not yet old enough for school when Christopher discovered that he had a growth in his abdomen nearly the size of a soccer ball. Surgery was immediate; the prognosis, poor. The best estimate was six months, and his doctors were so skilled that the prediction was accurate almost to the day.

Christopher and his wife had been close friends of their parish priest. Even before surgery, they had undertaken the beginning of their spiritual pilgrimage with his care and guidance. During Christopher's last six months their hour together was almost daily, much of it with Christopher alone, the two men exploring the life of prayer, the life of Jesus. They paid special attention to the burial service. Christopher planned every detail of the service that would to mark the end of his life among the friends and family who would gather in the church that day.

When the burial service did take place, the priest described in his homily the hours that had been spent with Christopher, what had been discussed and what had been planned by Christopher for this occasion, and why. After a careful retelling of those important conversations, the rector went on:

"Christopher came to a point in his life when he said, 'Yes.' Christopher came to a point in his life when he knew that the words of Jesus, 'I am the resurrection and the life; he who believes in me, though he die, yet shall he live,' were true. Christopher said to the Lord, 'I believe.'

"Now you and I know that those words might not be true. All of this that we have gathered to do here today might be a hoax, just a hoax.

"Christopher made a decision about that. Christopher said, 'Yes.'

"Now you, each of you, has to make a decision.
"Amen."

⁂   ⁂   ⁂

The homily looks to the future, not the unchanging future of immortality, a life without end, but to the new life that death and resurrection make possible. As Jesus said, "In my Father's house are many rooms." Death means the closing of one door, and the end, forever, of what took place in that room. Resurrection means moving into a new room and a new life.

ও   ও   ও

Charles leaned forward in the pew. He had been dreaming—for God's sake, how long had this been going on? Five minutes? An hour? Their old friend was resting his hands on either side of the pulpit, hunching over to peer at his notes as they had seen him do Sunday after Sunday for so many years—"poor sod, he looks terrible," Charles said to himself. "Glad it's not me."

But what was he saying about Nancy?

" . . . What shall we say and pray for Charles and Nancy? What for ourselves?

"Wherever home and family are for you, in that place, Jesus said, there are many spaces, rooms, houses. To that place he has gone to be for us when it is our time. There he is now with Nancy.

"We reach that place through death, Jesus' death, our death, death symbolized by the cross, always the cross. The cross is the experience of loss and deprivation we surely wish to avoid, as Jesus himself did on that night in the Garden of Gethsemane, just before he died. But we can not turn away. It is ours, this cross, this death, our very own. If we are wise, as few of us are, we reach out and embrace it. It hurts. Yet through that cross, we enter a new room, another place, one He has prepared for us.

"The cross is a frequent experience, one we come to know well, long before we stop breathing. If we turn away during those many opportunities we are offered before our longest journey that we make alone, then we come to know less and less. Nancy did not turn away.

Pain is inevitable, life is difficult, but through it, beyond it, there is promise—a new room, many mansions. 'If it were not so, would I have told you that I go to prepare a place for you?' That is the promise.

"The promise is unconditional love. Since Nancy's death three days ago, the time she left Charles and the many others whom she loved, we have all done a lot of thinking. Some of it has been serendipitous. Perhaps we have been thinking of the children—Nancy's and Charles's—and our own children, and how much they are loved by their parents. They do nothing to earn that love but it is theirs, by right, by birth. Everyone who knew Nancy experienced a real measure of that kind of unconditional love. Charles and their children knew it best, but we all glimpsed it. To know Nancy was to be grasped and not to be let go. No one would say she was perfect, but she embodied the love she had been given, and in her turn, she offered it to us who are here today.

"Nancy's loyalty and grace sprang from the depths. Now through death she has entered a new height, for she has grasped the cross and knows eternally the promise of unconditional love. What she gave away she now receives, even as she beholds the face of her Father in heaven. Amen."

ðŸ™¿   ðŸ™¿   ðŸ™¿

...Charles shifted in the pew and wished he could get up and go. He felt trapped, closed in, claustrophobic. If Nancy were in some other place, and she might well be, then he wanted to be there, and not here.

CHAPTER IV

In Assurance of Eternal Life 🍁

T HE HOMILY ENDS. The preacher turns, and all remain seated and silent for several moments before standing to proclaim what they believe at this time of loss.

   🍂 🍂 🍂

...Nancy, who had been distant, came closer. Blue was her color, and it surrounded him. He could smell her clean hair and the sun on her skin, feel his excitement as when he had returned home after a trip. Moments they had shared became available and distinct. He remembered the ancient fight about stuffing the Thanksgiving turkey. It seemed ridiculous now, and he turned from that to the Thursday morning last year when he had telephoned from his office and discovered that she was free for lunch. They had met like lovers, their conversation intense—first of her client of the morning and then Anne's move to Houston. He had wanted to take her home and to bed. Later. No more now. This was it.

For these past three days, time and time again, he had wished her alive. She was dead, dead, dead. Denial was the first enemy. He had seen it so often in students and colleagues, and told himself that when his time came, he would be right there to face his reality, own the moment.

But it was easier said than done. Only his sense of her presence now wasn't denial; she really was with him.

He thought of their wedding day, amazed to realize that despite the pain associated with this memory he could recall clear details: waking before dawn, the tension of the day, falling asleep together. One particular memory of the wedding ceremony dominated. As they stood before the altar, with no warning each began to cry. The reaction they couldn't help was hardly more powerful than their joy, but before every birth there is the death of what came before. Childhood, the familial relationships that had brought them to this moment, were no longer the same.

Now she was dead, yet still all around him was the same spirit, good sense, the maddening ability always to be right, to know what she believed and why.

ɜ   ɜ   ɜ

THE APOSTLES' CREED

Surrounded by loss, we are asked to stand and proclaim a faith which states that after death happens, each and every time it happens, there is always more. The more was given from God through Christ and becomes ours in baptism.

In the waters of baptism we are buried with Christ in his death. Life ends. Death happens, but through this death with Christ there is also resurrection from the bondage of sin into everlasting life. New life is born. Baptism states it clearly. Immersed in water, drowning, we die, yet the same water gives life. We are born to know endings, and through those endings, new beginnings. "For if we have been united with him in a death

like his, we shall certainly be united with him in a resurrection like his."

❧   ❧   ❧

...Shortly after marrying and beginning their first jobs,
the opportunity arose to buy a small piece of shorefront
property. They built a summer cottage, and there enjoyed
memorable parts of each summer as the children grew.

The natural beauty of the place and those summer
hours spent away from normal tensions and demands
created an aura about the cottage that came to be a
special center for their family life. Not that all was bliss,
living closely together day after day, and surrounded by
the inevitable tensions of jealousy and competition; still
and all, there was no other house so constant for them.
Moves were frequent, and professional opportunities
never allowed them to know any one other place as
home as they knew the physical surroundings of this
place.

Their oldest daughter's wedding came at a time of
major upheaval and change for each member of the
family. The one place to gather and celebrate new life
was the summer cottage where she had grown up. The
moment was crucial for the new couple and the entire
family. The time had come, for all of them, as it always
should, for new purpose and direction.

Change is the one constant. No matter where we live
on this earth, there is no abiding place. If we try to lay
claim to one single place or endeavor and make it permanent and immutable, then it will control us and make
us its prisoner. Once one chapter is concluded, it must be

left behind, for if we are captive to a single physical place or period of time, we shall die. Baptism is new life.

The property was sold.

       ❧   ❧   ❧

Death is inevitable, and we have the right and opportunity to meet it, face it, claim it, before it takes us. As Christians, we do so in the name and power and presence of Christ, the one who died so that we might live, the one who through baptism incorporates us into his death, so that we too shall partake of his resurrection.

Resurrection means a new life, a life consistent with the past, but separate and different. Eternal life in baptism is new life, not more of the same old thing. Eternal life is different from immortality.

       ❧   ❧   ❧

...Vacation, a few days in the sun, and too much time for television. The constant image of the friendly-looking, older, bald man kept reappearing as the story of his life was told over and over again.

Their four-year-old daughter did not understand, and it seemed a good time, in this protected and secluded environment where they were gathered as a family, to talk about death. The nice man was President Eisenhower. He was very old, had lived a long and very good life as a soldier, a hero, and then president, the leader of our whole country. Now he was dead, but only at the end of his life. Life ends in death, they told her, for President Eisenhower and for all of us.

The four-year-old burst into tears and cried uncontrollably. She did not want the nice man to be dead. If he died, then mummy and daddy would die, we would all die. Tell her it was not so. Make him not dead. She lost all ability to think sensibly, and would be consoled only with the assurance that we do not die. She hadn't even known who Eisenhower was. What had frightened her was the terrible realization that those she loved would die, and if that were true, then there had to be something more. The child demanded immortality, our most ancient fantasy.

The time had come to explain that, yes, there was something more. Death means that life is not the same, day after day.

"This year you started school. Remember that first day and how new and exciting everything was? You were the same little girl, but all of a sudden, everything was quite different, wasn't it? That's what it is like right now for President Eisenhower.

"Life is full of change, new beginnings. Death is one of those new beginnings. It happens to all of us, but because Jesus died for each of us, you and me and President Eisenhower, death is the beginning of something new and different."

In the assurance of eternal life given at Baptism, let us proclaim our faith and say,

I believe in God, the Father almighty,
  creator of heaven and earth.

...He always asked the question passionately, persuasively: "Will you help me believe in God?"

85

He meant it. Seventy years old when we first met, he was brilliant, honest and blunt. Even at a first meeting he would break through surface politeness with a remark such as, "You are some fella. I like you!" Then he would demand, one way or another, that you earn the affection he was so willing to offer.

For some—and I was not alone—his ability to be refreshingly and suprisingly honest was summed up this way: "Two regrets, two great regrets. Can't believe in God. Never got married. Now, that's a lot to miss in one lifetime. And see here. You've got 'em both. How about some help? Help me believe in God."

He meant it. But nothing helped. Talking about belief in God did not help, nor did the testimony of close friends. Neither the Eucharist nor faithful attendence in many different churches made a difference to him. Frequently on a Sunday morning he would acccompany lifelong friends, husband and wife, to their parish. When the time came, he would move to the rail with them and kneel beside them to receive the bread and wine. Later, at lunch she would be unable to contain herself any longer and burst out. "Bob, why do you do that? You shouldn't. You know you don't believe in God."

He would pause and then reply, "Of course I don't. But why not? It sure can't hurt, if He's not there. And, who knows, it just might help."

Finally, at the age of seventy-four, he took the craziest and most unusual step of his lifetime. He broke out of all his staid and normal and accepted practices, and all by himself undertook an adventure, a trip to China, the other side of the world. It was on that trip, while in China, that he met and fell in love with the one person he had sought throughout his life. They were married.

Then followed the five happiest, most fulfilled and expressive years of his life. They were years of discovery, none more powerful than the discovery that the God he had sought is a God of intimacy and love. Friendly, warm, outgoing as he had been with so many others, there had never been that one other, the person with whom he was one flesh. When she entered his life, a new dimension was created, and he saw for the first time that what he had known for seventy-four years was not all. What he had been given in marriage was more, far more, and it was not all. Now he knew without question.

He did not die at the end of his life. Well into his seventies, life was still beginning for him and his burial was the celebration of one who had been found and claimed by God.

I believe in Jesus Christ, his only Son, our Lord.
 He was conceived by the power of the Holy Spirit
 and born of the Virgin Mary.
He suffered under Pontius Pilate,
 was crucified, died, and was buried.
He descended to the dead.
On the third day he rose again.
He ascended into heaven,
 and is seated at the right hand of the Father.
He will come again to judge the living and the dead.

Jesus Christ was and is the incarnation—the presence in living flesh—of God. He came once. He comes again in personal power and presence, incarnate. God is with us constantly and in many forms. Daily, God is with us in flesh and blood, in our intimate connection with other living, breathing human beings, and our belief that this loving connection brings new life now and finds new form beyond death.

The personal presence of the living Lord changes our reality, invades the daily, making what is impossible possible, and what is absent present, turning unbelief into belief, a new reality. He comes again when, through the power of his presence, we are able to say, "I believe." The love of Jesus reaches out to us through the most significant people in our lives and embraces us in life and beyond death. Our realization of their belief in us is a reflection of the power of the love of Jesus present in our lives: changing us, directing us, making the impossible, possible.

ﺰ﮲   ﺰ﮲   ﺰ﮲

...Two long-time friends, now living in distant cities, created the opportunity to spend an evening together in old and familiar surroundings. Conversation, laughter, good food, wine, and it all seemed to be nearly over just as it began. Both men sensed that something remained to be said, and, before parting, they withdrew to a quiet corner of the room.

The younger man had in recent years become a dramatically successful and good artist. Each of the more than fifty works he had completed in these years had been purchased, some by serious collectors; three of his paintings already hung in prominent museums. Now he had something important to say.

"When I first came to you all those years ago, I was not a painter. Oh, I had a good education, and knew everything I needed to know. I had been taught well how to paint, but I was not yet a painter.

"Then we met. You believed in me. You believed that I was a painter and said to me, 'Go and paint.' I did, and so I became the painter you believed me to be. Tonight, I wanted to say thank you."

No more words. They embraced and parted.

ঽ৯·   ঽ৯·   ঽ৯·

Our glimpses of the incarnate Jesus are partial and fleeting, pale imitations of the powerful reality that is the Christ. There are, however, glimpses that make clear in a very brief moment what the power of the presence of the risen Christ is like. Finally, that power is beyond human comprehension, but when we see it, know it, and we do, then it is something like this.

ঽ৯   ঽ৯·   ঽ৯·

...George H. L. Mallory was last seen in 1924 hanging from a climbing line, surrounded by mist, in his unsuccessful assault on Mount Everest.

Earlier that same year, while preparing for the Everest attempt, Mallory and some friends trained on Mount Snowdon, the highest peak in Wales. As they neared the summit one afternoon, they stopped for a final rest and a smoke on a small ledge before completing the climb.

After supper, when Mallory reached for his pipe it was missing, and he remembered that he had left it on the ledge below. As dusk fell, he climbed down as they had come earlier, but returned by a shorter route. The next morning he and his party began the descent of Snowdon following the route Mallory had used when returning from the ledge. All were astounded by the difficulty of the climb he had made the previous evening.

When the next edition of the British Mountaineering Guide appeared, all precedent was broken by naming this new route after a person. It was described with these words:

"ROUTE 1A. A variation of Route 1 (see adjoining map). *This climb is totally impossible.* It was performed once in failing light by Mr. George H. L. Mallory."

I believe in the Holy Spirit,
  the holy catholic Church,
  the communion of saints,
  the forgiveness of sins,
  the resurrection of the body,
  and the life everlasting. Amen.

God the Holy Spirit is our experience of wholeness, the realization that our very own life, like a good novel, has a plot. The Holy Spirit is the presence of vitality and meaning in the daily round and common task, the clear interrelation of God and daily life.

Concidences are God's way of remaining anonymous. There is no such thing as coincidence, only the presence of the Holy Spirit. The curious, even unexplained intersection of events, common and uncommon, bespeak the presence of God. Trivial conversation does not exist. All our words carry meaning. The hand of God is ever present in all experience, especially, even particularly, the daily, the simple, the mundane and the unexpected. For those who have eyes to see and ears to hear, God is everywhere at work, never distant, always present.

The way in which God is most constantly and powerfully present is in resurrection—making what was dead new and alive.

~ ~ ~

...He was one of the last to arrive at the funeral, and the church was already full. Seated in the last pew, he noticed his father, whom he had not seen for over a year, sitting alone on the side aisle. The son's adrenaline began to flow, his pulse quickened, a tear started to form. Each man pretended not to see the other.

The coffin passed just by his shoulder, so close he could have reached out and touched it, and he focused all his attention on the memories it carried. The old priest had been a model and mentor. Time and time again he had stood up front, exactly where his coffin had been placed, at the crossing. There he stood and said, "God is everywhere, everywhere." Then he would stretch out his right arm toward the congregation and move it back and forth, back and forth. "God is always present, part of all our lives, here, right now, tomorrow, always." The hand never stopped moving back and forth, back and forth, defining a great horizontal space that included everyone who listened.

"But once upon a time, God came in a special way. He came down into our lives, your lives." His outstretched hand would start moving up and down, up and down, up and down. "God came once, on the cross, and He comes again. He comes when you meet the cross in your life," and now he would combine his two motions, his arm moving first back and forth and then up and down.

91

"This is where we live, my friends, right here, at the crossing."

His burial had brought a large company of old friends together. The service was almost over. In a fleeting, unconscious moment, father and son caught each others' eye, as each rose, simultaneously, to walk forward to the crossing to receive the bread and wine. The distance between them closed as they moved closer to the rail. Conversation was not possible, but as if by chance, they found their way to the crossing together. They stopped and turned to face one another, and then knelt, side by side, hands outstretched, to receive.

THE PRAYERS OF THE PEOPLE

The Prayers of the People, part of every Eucharist, are intercessions, a series of prayers offered on behalf of others. These particular intercessions follow the Creed, as now we prepare to approach the altar and celebrate the presence of the risen Christ in bread and wine. The Burial of the Dead includes specific intercessions for the person who has died and for those who mourn. More than this, they are prayers that identify Jesus as a person well acquainted with sorrow and death, one who knew compassion and the depth of loss.

For our brother (sister) N., let us pray to our Lord Jesus Christ who said, "I am Resurrection and I am Life."

Prayer offered at the time of death is centered in and summoned by the power of the resurrection. Here we pray to Jesus, who is the resurrection.

The life and death and new life of Jesus the Christ established resurrection as a different dimension of human existence. In the name and power of Jesus and the resurrection, we pray for him who has died. Why? We pray because we mourn; we pray because we want to be connected; we pray to establish the bond of prayer between the one who has died and new life in Christ. Prayer is a link, a bond, the basis of communication, the network that binds us together with God and with one another. Our prayer reaches out and includes the one whom we loved and is now no longer with us, and raises him to the presence of new life in Christ.

Lord, you consoled Martha and Mary in their distress; draw near to us who mourn for N., and dry the tears of those who weep.

Martha and Mary and their brother Lazarus were Jesus' close friends. Lazarus was sick and dying. The sisters sent for Jesus to help them, but by the time he arrived, Lazarus was dead. Jesus did several things: he offered the consolation of his presence and friendship; he proclaimed the power of resurrection and life; he joined with them in their sorrow, he wept, and then he raised Lazarus from the dead. At the story's center is Jesus' open and heartfelt sorrow: "Jesus wept."

This, the shortest verse in the Bible, is one of its most powerful. Soon after the moment it describes, Jesus raised Lazarus from the dead, demonstrating that tears release great power. Never casual, tears express the most powerful emotion of which we are capable. But tears are never an end in themselves.

Tears provide the means for healing, restoration, new life, and unless there are tears, nothing happens, no power is released. Tears open the way for new possibilities. It is when the tears of those who weep are dried that healing begins. Healing takes many forms, bears many marks; often it begins with release, and is marked by laughter. Tears have great power. Some of their power isolates, insulates the one who weeps. When those tears have been dried, then laughter joins one to another. Laughter is new life, the healer that dries the tears of pain and replaces them with joy.

    æ æ æ

...She picked up the telephone. It was a long-distance call with a terrible connection, but she could make out the hysterical voice of her new sister-in-law. Her brother, her only living relative, was dead. The hospital testing of the day before, carried out one year after a serious heart attack, had been fatal. Her only living relative, a new husband and recently a father—dead.

She slammed the telephone into its cradle and threw herself onto the hotel bed, sobbing. The children were quiet and scared, knowing what had happened, but confused and frightened. Her audible cries were incoherent, expressing fright and grief. She was alone, the sole survivor of her family. No one was left. The door to her past had been slammed, and she was alone.

Her husband had retreated to a far corner. He never was any good in a crisis, but something had to be done. After long silence, with the only sound her sobs, muffled by the pillow, he moved to her side, knelt, and smoothed the coverlet around her. Then he put his face very close to hers and whispered, "You must be very still and quiet. Don't move a muscle. You're descended from a very rare

94

strain, special, so special that not a single one remains except you!"

No reply. Only sobs and more sobs. He continued.

"We must care of you. You've got to take care of yourself. You come from a long line of croakers. Your family is especially good at dying. Early and untimely death must not be your fate. Be still."

She turned over. Her sobbing stopped. "Why don't you shut up!"

"No, no, no, I can't. Just think, if you go and croak, what would you care? You wouldn't even feel it. We'll be the ones left behind, all alone. Think of us and then lie still." She stirred. "No, you mustn't move even a muscle. You're the last of the great croakers. We can't lose you now."

The faintest hint of a smile touched her lips. The children didn't understand, started to scream, ran over to their father and tried to pummel him on the back. "Stop it, stop it, daddy. Don't be mean to mummy."

"I'm not being mean. Not mean at all. You've got to help. Your mother is the last of the great croakers, and we can't lose her now. She has just got to lie still, very still, right here, and you and I will wait on her every whim."

The children's protests faded. It began to work. Over and over again he repeated. "Lie still. You are the last of the great croakers. We can't lose you now. Lie very, very still."

She couldn't help it, and she did start to laugh. The children joined her, and so did he. All of them repeating, "The last of the great croakers...the last of the great croakers..."

Surrounded by death, through the tears, came laughter and through the laughter a palpable physical bond.

You wept at the grave of Lazarus, your friend; comfort us in our sorrow.

"Jesus wept." These words mark the powerful expression of Jesus' presence at the tomb of his dead friend Lazarus. He has come too late to find Lazarus alive, too late, not by accident, but quite deliberately, the text from the Gospel of John states, to allow Jesus to proclaim the power of the new life he brings, a new life rooted in love.

But then, in spite of himself, grief overwhelms Jesus, and grief brings new life. Sorrow is painful, but without it we are not whole. The strength that Jesus discovers comes when he grieves. Grief is powerful, and grief brings power. New life begins only after death. Grief is that process by which the loss is transformed into new life and strength.

For the most part, however, we steel ourselves against grief, shut it out, avoid it, block it, or, at the very least, we struggle not to reveal it to any one, even to the one we love the most. When we hide our grief, we damage and diminish that love, and when we allow grief, new life begins.

          ۯ   ۯ   ۯ

...The brilliant October morning, colorful, cold, full of the promise of winter, drew him to work early. He reached his office, and realized that someone was already present, sitting on the couch and waiting for him. A new colleague, they had worked together only a few weeks.

Pretending surprise, he realized as he entered that he had known that one day, one day soon, he would find Sam here. Sam's marriage had been over for some time—

he had read it in their initial conversation and his first meeting with Sam's wife. He knew why he had come. There was no need to speak. Sam blurted, "I'm sorry, but I've just got to see you. I have to talk to someone."

The moment was full of pain but at the same time it seemed natural, inevitable. "She's leaving me. This morning she went on and on and on. I couldn't make her stop. She had to tell me, again and again, about how they'd made love. Then she said she wouldn't be home for supper because she would be with him—for the night. It felt like she was stabbing me, right here in the stomach with a knife, and then turning it.

Sam stopped talking as suddenly as he had begun and burst into tears. He cried openly, uncontrollably.

"She has no idea how much I love her....She only wants to hurt me....It hurts so much....Oh, God, how it hurts. Why me? Why me?" Tears ran down both cheeks and fell on the coffee table in front of him.

"Have you ever cried like this with her?"

"Never. I couldn't. If I ever did, she'd know how vulnerable I am. You don't know her. She's a bitch. Pure bitch. All she cares about is controlling every man she's ever known. That's what she's done with me and with her father over all that alcohol bullshit. But I love her. God, I love her."

After a while his tears stopped. The two men sat in silence. Then as each rose and shook hands, an unexpected thing happened. It happened without words, and it was only the fact that each looked long and hard into the eyes of the other and promised to stay in touch. They did.

You raised the dead to life; give to our sister (brother) eternal life.

You promised paradise to the thief who repented; bring your brother (sister) to the joys of heaven.

All of the persons who surrounded Jesus on the day he died—the thieves, the disciples, his mother and the other women—represent us. That's why they were there then, and why they are there now, for all of us have remained constant. Identification with them is not easy. The thief was hung out to die: nameless, forgotten and unknown, save to his own pain and loneliness. Not one other person there knew what it was like to be inside his skin, except the one who hung next to him.

When all is said and done, what each of us craves more than anything else is for one other person—just one—to know what it means to be inside our skin. Paradise may be many things, but one way we experience it is through someone else knowing, really knowing, what it means to be me. When that happens, we know something of heaven. Heaven is when I am known as I am, really known. Heaven is when there is no more isolation and loneliness and pain. Heaven is having a name and being remembered. Jesus promised paradise to the thief who repented, and that is what he promises to you and me.

This promise of eternal life is not merely for when we die. It is for now. Eternal life is whenever we are known, truly known, remembered, and valued. That does not happen often, but when it does, then we have tasted the meaning of eternal life.

ॐ   ॐ   ॐ

..."I hope I go to heaven, but I probably won't. Why should I? I've already had my lovely time right here, and I have plenty to be ashamed of. But maybe your Uncle Henry will put in a good word for me. Do you think he might?"

"I can't believe I'm hearing this. You mean to tell me that your little tiny view of heaven is some place where you are in or you are out depending on the quality of your miserable little life here and now? You have the gall to believe that heaven might be in any way measured by who you are and what you have done?"

"Don't be so self-righteous. You known very well that that is the way a lot of people think."

"Sure. A lot of people think that way, or rather they don't think. If heaven is, and it is, then it is the be-all and end-all, the sum total of human experience in all of time. Heaven is the crowning creation of all that God was and is and will be. So if heaven is heaven, then what possible difference could it make who you are? Or that once you lived and now you are dead? You may want to believe that you are important, but that doesn't matter much in heaven."

"Then what does matter, if I don't matter?"

"God....Heaven has to do with God and our relationship to God, now and then. The only thing that makes it even remotely possible is Christ, and the fact that Christ died for you. Nothing else matters. Forget about Henry...what matters is your relationship to Jesus."

"And what am I supposed to do about that?"

"You don't have to do a thing. It's all been done. You only have to be. Be the person God made you to be. Be responsive to that love. Be aware and responsive to the fact that Christ died for you that you might have life in heaven, even with Uncle Henry!"

She (he) was nourished with your Body and Blood; grant her (him) a place at the table in your heavenly kingdom.

The table of the heavenly kingdom is no different from our breakfast table or our dinner table. If we want to know something about our experience of the heavenly banquet, we should take a closer look at the meals we eat at our own table. Life experience is consistent. There are no surprises. Sartre was correct when he described hell as the place where all were blind, just as C. S. Lewis described hell as a place of distance so great that no one could talk with anyone else.

The great banquet table of the heavenly kingdom will be very like the table around which we gather every day with those we love. The world we create for ourselves with one another, with those whom we embrace or those we avoid, will be the world in which we shall dwell for eternity.

❧   ❧   ❧

...Summer after summer, when the children were still small, they traveled together as a family. A wise and older woman named those moments when she said, "You are buying memories." The memories were engraved in each of them, and years later one child could start on a given day of a certain summer, describe the day and the place and the surroundings, and then each would pick up in turn to tell of what happened the next day, and the next and the next.

One particular memory blended with others: the memory of picnics, picnics in graveyards. They decided on their very first journey out of Paris that they would purchase bread and cheese and paté and fruit and Orangina and wine and then drive until they found the best place for a picnic. It turned out to be a thirteenth-century country church surrounded by a small cemetery. They stopped, got out, and ate and drank. It was a moment that came to be repeated in different ways, day after day, speaking of a profound reality that included delicious food, the activities of the cows always nearby, the family fights of that morning, and what had been seen and savored that was new and exciting.

Of all those picnics, only one was eaten at a table, not in a graveyard. The day was fair, their first time in the Loire Valley. Driving along the river, they had turned and driven, up, up, to sit in the small park adjacent to the walls of Saumur that rose next to them, steep and tall. Sitting around a white wooden table in white wooden chairs, the twelve-year-old girl sat across from them munching reflectively, strangely silent, the sun shining on her blond pigtails and reflected in her large round tortoise-shell glasses.

As she continued to munch, the thought within her grew and grew until it was ready. She spoke. "You know, when you're on a trip you're always looking for something. Then you realize what you're looking for is home."

Comfort us in our sorrows at the death of our brother (sister); let our faith be our consolation, and eternal life our hope.

It might turn out to be mother or Uncle Bert or Great Aunt Alice. At every funeral there is always someone who keeps repeating, usually at the wrong time, "Whenever God shuts a door, He opens a window." These may not be the exact words, but close enough. They probably seemed hackneyed and trite and are better left unsaid.

Yet they are true. Everything comes to an end: every life, every friendship, every job, every day, and when it ends, another begins.

> Will they stop,
> Will they stand there for a moment, perhaps before
>   some shop where they have gone so many times
> (Stand with the same blue sky above them and the
>   stones, so often walked, beneath)
>
> Will it be a day like this—
> As though there could be such a day again—
> And will their concerns still be about the same,
> And will the feeling still be this that you have felt so many
> times,
> Will they meet and stop and speak, one perplexed and one
> aloof.
>
> Saying: Have you heard,
> Have you heard,
> Have you heard about the death?
>
> And will that be all?
> On a day like this, with motors streaming through the
>   fresh parks, the streets alive with casual people,
> And everywhere, on all of it, the brightness of the sun.
>
> Will it be like this, and will that be all?

ða   ða   ða

...The June evening was pleasantly warm, the air soft, the light lingering, the proper moment for the goodbye party. We were being fêted at the end of four full and happy years as rector and wife of a young, lively parish.

The time had come to undertake a new and quite different ministry. This meant we had to say goodbye and move on a good deal sooner than any one expected.

We stood together with the host and hostess at the entrance to the garden and greeted each guest. When everyone had arrived, together we milled about casually, and then sat under torches on the large sloping lawn for strawberries and champagne. Then it was time for speeches of farewell and gifts to mark the occasion. The moment was bittersweet, full of happy memories yet still sad.

The evening came to an end, and it was the very end. Tomorrow, the moving van. We were leaving. They were staying. It is never easy to say good bye. We all know we have to someday, but if it is final, then there is regret, even anger.

We approached our hostess with warmth and gratitude to make our farewells. As we did so she turned her back on us, and as she walked toward the house said coldly, "I hope you come to regret this evening."

> A Death blow is a Life blow to Some
> Who till they died, did not alive become—
> Who had they lived, had died but when
> They died, Vitality begun.

ða   ða   ða

The Prayers of the People now conclude with the following collect.

Father of all, we pray to you for N., and for all those whom we love but see no longer.

103

Those whom we love we shall always continue to see, especially if their absence is caused by death.

We see them in sleep. Those recently dead, whose love we are unable to live without, appear and reappear in our dreams, at first nightly, then less frequently, speaking, acting, and responding as they did in moments of past intimacy.

We talk with them in prayer, at the Eucharist, at every time we are willing to summon their memory and presence to accompany us before God. The power of prayer is never restricted to any one time or occasion, but it is deepened when we pray at stated and practiced times and places.

We know their presence in a treasured possession that remains with us, evoking memory of a moment, a conviction, a statement. Each morning when I put on my father's watch, I put on his belief in time and beauty and the opportunity to fill each moment. When I sit at my desk, my father's desk, I am mindful of his belief in the "small change of brotherly love"—the necessity to write letters that touch and heal, as he did every day of his life.

We bear them in our body, behind our face, in stance and walk. Each of us is a necropolis, one who embodies those special persons who have touched and shaped and loved us. Family resemblance, common traits and interests, though important, are only one part of this continuing reality. We carry our family members with us in our body and in the very expression of our souls, and as we do so, they are with us.

Thomas Merton wrote that as he grew toward the new openness that resulted in his conversion, in one special and memorable moment, his father, dead one year, was present with him, just as if he were in the same room, as they walked and talked together.

Thomas Wolfe wrote on the occasion of the death of his brother Ben:

> We can believe in the nothingness of life,
> we can believe in the nothingness of death
> and life after death—
> but who can believe in the nothingness of Ben?

Those whom we love are always near, in death as in life.

❧   ❧   ❧

...The dream was vivid and in full color. In the dream he entered his father's office, the office he had visited frequently in childhood. Miss Barr, the secretary, told him to go right on in, but when he opened the inner door he did not see his father seated behind his desk, but lying in a raised hospital bed and attended by his mother. Father was unshaven and wearing his favorite bathrobe, the bathrobe that now hung in his son's closet. Walking into the room, he drew near his father's bed. They held hands and talked. His father looked and spoke and smelled just as he did when they had last met and talked, only now he lay in a hospital bed placed in the very office where competition and stress had killed him thirty-three years ago.

Not until three weeks later, describing his dream in the midst of a family meal, did his own daughter point out that the dream had occurred at precisely the hour and minute when his father had died thirty-three years earlier.

Grant to them eternal rest. Let light perpetual shine upon them.

Curious. When I was little, I was afraid of the dark. Perhaps you were, too. Perhaps we both are still.

What frightens us is that there is nothing there. On that one night when you were absolutely sure there was a monster under the bed, and you gathered up all your courage and turned on your light and got out of bed and down on your hands and knees and looked—you know what you saw? Nothing! What you were afraid of was nothing.

Coming from the basement upstairs to the kitchen, I would carefully arrange the darkness to fall only behind me, where I had just been, leaving the nothingness behind me all by itself. Then I would run ahead of it as fast as I could go, believing that if I had a head start, it would remain alone, below in the dark.

The monster under my bed dwelt in darkness. When the light went on, and we got down on our hands and knees to peer in under to see what was there, the monster was gone. Perhaps he was afraid of the light.

It was God who made the light to mark the day, yet the darkness and the light are both alike to him. Not for you and me. We do not want to dwell in darkness, but in the light. The light of love and joy and peace and friendship.

May the souls of all the departed, through the mercy of God, rest in peace. Amen.

CONFESSION OF SIN

Let us confess our sins against God and our neighbor.

Most merciful God,
we confess that we have sinned against you
in thought, word, and deed,
by what we have done,
and by what we have left undone.
We have not loved you with our whole heart;
we have not loved our neighbors as ourselves.
We are truly sorry and we humbly repent.
For the sake of your Son Jesus Christ,
have mercy on us and forgive us;
that we may delight in your will,
and walk in your ways,
to the glory of your Name. Amen.

The Confession of Sin understands that human life is potentially one seamless fabric, one tapestry. This potential, however, has been destroyed by sin. Life as we know it is fragmented, fractured, broken apart by acts, conscious and unconscious, known and unknown, intelligent and stupid, willful and casual. The result is isolation, our isolation that we experience as loneliness and separation, created by sin, our sin, the sin that involves all people.

Sin is the drive of every one of us to put ourself in the center of the world, and as much as each of us is able, to draw the world into and around us. Whether unintentionally or by design, human beings do not want to accept the world as it is given, but strive to place their mark upon it, to mold the world around them to their own uses and needs, to make all we touch, see, handle and use serve us. Some are more able to do this than others, and they become leaders not through the desire to serve others, but to be served. This is called sin, and before we look upon it with either amazement or horror, we must simply acknowledge it as a fact.

We can neither avoid sin nor, in any real sense, atone for it. Sin holds us in its grip, and the inevitable result of this grip is death. Paul said, "For the wages of sin is death, but the free gift of God is eternal life in Christ Jesus our Lord."

Life, as described in the two opening chapters of Genesis, once upon a time was immortal; it went on forever, undisturbed and unchanged. Our unwillingness to accept the world as created, but instead to mold it to serve our individual purposes, changed that. As a result, it is impossible for life to continue in a world that human beings as individuals and groups have molded to serve different purposes. Conflict ensues and death results. The seamless fabric is rent asunder and the pattern of the tapestry of God disrupted. Sin brings death.

"The wages of sin is death." The examples are many and obvious. Nations want their own way, beguiled by the demonic leadership of a Hitler or a Stalin. The world must conform to their expectations, and the attempt to bring this to pass results in death, the death of millions upon millions of people. More subtly, tycoons and their followers want the earth to serve their own ends. So what matters are individual goals, not the dangers of erosion, pollution, stockpiling of nuclear waste, acid rain, the permanent extinction of hundreds of species, and our potential for extinguishing all life on the face of the earth:

permanent death. Those worries are for others, those who will come later.

Statistical examples are just as clear as individual ones. More than 50,000 times each year in the United States the self-will and wanton destruction of the drunken driver kills or maims an innocent person. Drinking under other circumstances, while personally destructive, does not impinge on others in such a blatant way, yet few drunks take thought for the wishes and rights of others, and these acts of sin result in death.

ஃ   ஃ   ஃ

...Susan had put away her high school yearbook photograph some years ago, no longer comfortable with her shy beauty, the suggestion of a smile, hair pulled back, turned under in a pageboy. She liked even less the memory of the accompanying biography: minor clubs in sophomore and junior years, nothing really to show for those four years, and the concluding statement that she would attend the local business college.

Tom hardly ever mentioned his years in school and college, despite the fact that he had skated his way from a second-rate high school into a good college and graduate school. Although he had charm, good looks, and athletic ability, these never seemed enough to make him feel good enough about being Tom. Two days after graduation he had married his college sweetheart—more to give him confidence than from love. The marriage ended the day their daughter entered kindergarten.

He met Susan years later during a February skiing weekend at the same Vermont inn. They married in June, and the marriage began with promise. Both had seen much of the world, and each was professionally established. There was travel, financial rewards, a constantly renewable source of friends, change, fresh challenge. Susan chronicled the record of their common life in four big scrapbooks, one for each year, now stored in the dim recesses of the hall closet. Photographs of their trips— large groups, smiling faces, never the same, cocktail parties, sunlit beaches, expensive clothes. The pace was fast, taking in many different people, as each continued to move ahead.

Their lives allowed for less and less time together. Soon it made good sense for Tom to live in another city, more convenient to his life and career, while Susan remained behind in their new house, surrounded by her work, her friends. Weekends were spent together—at first every weekend, then every other, later once a month. Now little remained of or for Tom in the house they once had shared. No one—not Tom, not Susan, not any friend, near or far—could pinpoint the moment the marriage ended. It just did.

ɘ̀   ɘ̀   ɘ̀

...It had all been so simple. To be sure, it took time, but the process of undercutting the president of the company, subtly at first, then more blatantly, had come naturally and he did it well. Easy access to the Board of Directors and certain key clients had helped, and both were part of his job as administrative assistant to the president. He had allowed himself a full five years to complete the task. Progress was cumulative. The circle of confidantes grew, conversations about their leader's performance more and more frequent. His goal came closer and closer.

110

His final achievement came suddenly. A specially con-
vened executive session from which the president was
excluded, and where he was a special guest. One vote,
and it was all over. He was now in charge.

What he never foresaw or even dreamed happened
quite as suddenly five years later. Another executive session, and he was out. "The punishment for wanting the
wrong thing in life is that you get it."

ﻭ   ﻭ   ﻭ

Sin brings death. Not merely for a chosen few, for those
who are especially self-centered and avaricious—nor for
those whose single objective in life is to further their am-
bitions. The confluence of sin and death involves and en-
velops all of us. Not one of us is exempt. The web of sin
wraps around us and draws us inexorably toward death.
It does not matter if we succeed or fail at the tasks set
before us. Sin is present, and it leads to death.

*Almighty God have mercy on you, forgive you all your sins
through our Lord Jesus Christ, strengthen you in all goodness,
and by the power of the Holy Spirit keep you in eternal life.
Amen.*

If we confess our sin, our own grievous sin, and ask to
be forgiven, then we have absolution and new possibility
and new life—eternal life.

Since 1970 Elisabeth Kübler-Ross has been engaged in
teaching and writing about death and dying. The direction of her work has found a new form of expression in
more recent years and is now centered exclusively on the
necessity and importance of forgiveness. Each of us

comes to terms with dying, Kubler-Ross believes, when we face our own unfinished business, those parts of life experience that cry out for forgiveness. She counsels that each person must let out the suppressed frustration and rage in order to live with love and not hate. "The moment you forgive yourself," she claims, "you will never feel guilt again."

But how do I forgive myself for being myself? I can't. It's impossible. The person I am, just like the person you are, is caught up in the power of sin. Sin excludes love and leads to death, but there is a more powerful forgiveness than self-forgiveness.

Each of us is touched and healed by the forgiveness of God. After we acknowledge our need for forgiveness in the ritual of confession, we receive absolution, the pronouncement of forgiveness that is given from God through Christ.

       🙜   🙜   🙜

...Alexis, Baron von Roenne, a colonel in the German army who was opposed to National Socialism, did not take part in the attempt of July 20, 1944 on Hitler's life, but his ties to those who did led to his imprisonment and execution. Shortly before his death, he wrote his wife:

> I have no part nor guilt in what has happened, no matter what may be said afterwards. All else is of no importance in comparison with this. However, this exceedingly grave time has brought me an enormous gain. I have returned completely into the arms of our Lord and Savior, which I had often enough forgotten in the pressure of events. I spend nearly all my free time in prayer, a prayer for strength in myself in the face of everything that is to come, and for blessing and help for you, my most beloved, and for the children. And

112

so I sense so clearly the gift of fortitude that has come to me that I embark on everything with the joyful assurance that it can end nowhere but close to the heart of God, in eternal peace. Then indeed all that has gone before seems quite unimportant and should not concern you at all. At each moment, my inner eye will see behind anything only the open arms of my Lord and Savior. My firm comfort and foundation are the sayings, "And him that cometh to me I will in no wise cast out" and "Though your sins be scarlet, they shall be white as snow," and then the many other pregnant expressions of God's love as the profoundest reason for this attitude towards us.

On the day he was executed, October 12, 1944 in Berlin-Plotzensee, he wrote this final letter to his wife:

My dearest beloved: In a moment now I shall be going home to our Lord in complete calm and in the certainty of salvation. My thoughts are with you, with all of you, with the very greatest love and gratitude.

As my last wish, I entreat you to cling to Him and to have full confidence in Him; He loves you.

Any decision you may take for all of you, after prayer, has my complete sanction and my blessing. If only you knew with what inconceivable loyalty He is standing by my side at this moment, you would be armored and calm for all of your difficult life. He will give you strength for everything.

I bless both of our beloved children, and include them in my last ardent prayer. May the Lord let His countenance shine upon them and lead them home.

Heartfelt greetings and thanks to my beloved Mama, to your parents and my brothers and sisters. May they, safe-guarded by Him, survive even difficult times in our ardently beloved fatherland.

To you, my very dearest of all, belong my ardent love and thanks to the last moment and until our blessed reunion.

God keep you.

CHAPTER V

A Foretaste of Your Heavenly Banquet

At The Eucharist

"COME AND HAVE BREAKFAST." Charles heard her words again, words of good morning and welcome that had come to mean goodbye. Did they come from deep within him, or were they being repeated strangely and mysteriously right now? He was not certain.

He was sure that he saw Nancy sitting next to him at the dining room table, purple lilacs in her favorite Staffordshire bowl. Outside rain struck the window panes, the grass unusually green, heavy with moisture, the morning darkened by rain. Before eating, he had reached for her hand. They touched and spoke words of grace and thanks.

The meal was juice, oatmeal, toast, an ordinary meal that began most of their ordinary days. So many memories were summoned by the taste of a fresh orange, dry toast, lumpy oatmeal, memories that embodied much of his life, and here and now, all of their marriage. The memories were not only of what had been or even might have been. Those words "Come and have breakfast" proclaimed something more, stretching out through time and space, touching and bringing into focus many people.

Two memories were most vivid. The first, painful and empty, was the memory of all those breakfasts when Nancy and the children sat down at the table without him. He was always somewhere else—too busy, too important, spending hour upon hour in the university library or his study, writing, grading papers, conferring with colleagues, traveling, presenting papers, always somewhere else, rushing out, leaving home and family, forth into the world to respond to his own ambition, leaving behind his empty chair at the end of the table.

The other memory was happier, and it was indelible. Just married, the two of them had borrowed a friend's cabin on a lake. For five wonderful days, each morning they had cooked a late breakfast together and carried it outside to eat at a wooden picnic table beside the water. Whether they sat in silence or talked and joked, the birds were always there, everywhere, perched on the wooden bench, hopping onto the table, pecking at the muffins. The memory of their breakfasts had never left him—it was as fresh and sharp as the taste of orange juice.

Now the pain of this moment, the depth of his love, the power of his longing for Nancy all met together in the memory of their final breakfast, and then all the meals when they had gathered at their table: supper with the children, Sunday morning before church, ordinary days, special days—Christmas, Easter, Thanksgiving, birthdays. The memorable and the daily had been so often marked by meals. Conversations and convictions shared in this setting were still his, not fleeting, not ephemeral but present. The past was past, but the memory that surrounded those meals was more than a memory.

అ   అ   అ

> When they got out on land, they saw a charcoal fire there, with fish lying on it, and bread. Jesus said to them, "Bring some of the fish that you have just caught." So Simon Peter went abroad and hauled the net ashore, full of large fish, a hundred and fifty-three of them; and although there were so many, the net was not torn. Jesus said to them, "Come and have breakfast."

"Come and have breakfast." Jesus' words announce the final meal with his disciples, according to the Gospel of John. Death and resurrection have taken place, and there is one final meeting, marked by a meal: breakfast.

Throughout the Bible, again and again, the most significant and memorable meetings with the Lord are marked by meals. These meals pull together persons and events, central strands, interweaving time and place, holding up and making continually accessible what is finally the most important thing. Meals nourish, but meals also sustain us through tragedy and across time.

The Eucharist is such a meal. It is a meal that deals with the issues of death and life, marked by one particular death, an event that happened once. Through it, we find new life that lasts forever. Perhaps we have been at a Eucharist before, perhaps we attend faithfully week after week, but this particular one, the Eucharist of the Burial of the Dead, is different. We come surrounded by death, to be met by the God who died for us and with us and offers us new life that is the foretaste of the heavenly banquet. And this is precisely what happens. When death is present, the Lord who said "Come and have breakfast" joins us in this Eucharist offered to him in the name of our beloved, who has died. The little, the daily deaths overwhelm us when we awake each morning, but we find ways to avoid them, insist on their insignificance, and make them manageable. So too the life of one single human being may not be significant in the total sweep of the universe, but that life, whether ours or the life of the one we love now dead, has unique value in the economy of God. The Eucharist makes this clear and allows us to look at life and death in the context of Jesus's death and resurrection and to know that whenever death happens, new life begins.

THE GREAT THANKSGIVING

Celebrant	*Lift up your hearts.*
People	*We lift them to the Lord.*
Celebrant	*Let us give thanks to the Lord our God.*
People	*It is right to give him thanks and praise.*

It is right, and a good and joyful thing, always and everywhere to give thanks to you, Father Almighty, Creator of heaven and earth. Through Jesus Christ our Lord; who rose victorious from the dead, and comforts us with the blessed hope of everlasting life. For to your faithful people, O Lord, life is changed, not ended; and when our mortal body lies in death, there is prepared for us a dwelling place eternal in the heavens. Therefore we praise you, joining our voices with Angels and Archangels and with all the company of heaven, who for ever sing this hymn to proclaim the glory of your Name:

Holy, holy, holy Lord, God of power and might, heaven and earth are full of your glory.

Hosanna in the highest.
Blessed is he who comes in the name of the Lord
Hosanna in the highest.

The Great Thanksgiving, this action of Eucharist, begins with the words of the Sursum Corda, "Lift up your hearts" and moves through the Proper Preface for the Burial of the Dead and the Preface to the Sanctus, "Holy, holy, holy."

These are central and ancient words that come from the beginnings of the Christian faith. It is this moment in the Eucharist when we gather, by word and act and tradition, with all those persons, known and unknown, remembered and forgotten, who have gone before us into eternal life. Here we summon them to gather with us in the Eucharist, our act of thanksgiving that joins us with those who have died. This act takes place at every celebration of the Eucharist, but it happens more pointedly now. Here and now we are bound to the dead—through and at and in this meal.

≈·   ≈·   ≈·

...The news reached me first at the end of a late night meeting, a casual, almost off-handed remark. "Have you heard? David has cancer. He's already in the hospital."

The next morning I went to see him. He was sitting on top of the hospital bed, fully clothed, eating breakfast. He laughed when I came around the door, and his smile stopped me dead in my tracks. When I crossed the room to shake his hand and replied to his grin with some off-handed banter, he took my hand and said, "I don't want to die, but I'm going to." David never minced words.

119

He remained in the hospital for most of the next four months. Short stints at home, then back for treatment. He was confined to one spot, always available, and our conversations, usually twice each week, were lengthy. Early on he was much like himself, but when the chemotherapy took hold, he became weak and nauseous. But even when his tongue was thick, his speech slow and clouded, our talk continued, mostly about death and love, punctuated by frequent laughter that bonded and relaxed us. It seemed to open the way for candor and helped lead us to prayer. The last time I saw David alive was shortly after his final dose of chemotherapy. Just as the prayer ended, and we both said "Amen," he threw up all over his pillow. All we could do was laugh.

Then the miracle happened. David recovered. Life resumed its normal pattern, and our time together was over. We had been brought close by death; life brought distance. No one, at least not I, expected what happened next. In the summer he contracted a viral infection, and died three days later.

Despite the hot, hazy weather, vacation, and the dog days of summer, there was not an empty seat in the great church when David's service began. The words of the Preface—"joining our voices with Angels and Archangels and with all the company of heaven"—made David's presence palpable, and when I approached the altar to kneel and receive the bread and wine, he was there with me. Now he is with me at every Eucharist when all the saints are summoned to gather with us around the altar to celebrate the death that brings new life.

THE EUCHARISTIC PRAYER

We give thanks to you, O God, for the goodness and love which you have made known to us in creation; in the calling of Israel to be your people; in your Word spoken through the prophets; and above all in the Word made flesh, Jesus your Son. For in these last days you sent him to be incarnate from the Virgin Mary, to be the Savior and Redeemer of the world. In him, you have delivered us from evil, and made us worthy to stand before you. In him you have brought us out of error into truth, out of sin into righteousness, out of death into life.

When all is said and done, this is the promise each of us is given through life in Christ. We are brought out of error into truth, out of sin into righteousness, out of death into life.

We are grasped, summoned, called, whoever or wherever we may be, to be Christ's here and now, in this life. But first, in the beginning, our beginning, we take little thought of the future, living as Christ taught us for each day, one day at a time. Death is not real as long as we hang on to the belief that we are immortal, that life goes on forever. Sooner or later, however, that doesn't work. One day at a time is not sufficient. Death becomes more and more real, especially when we discover that the marks of sin and death touch us long before we stop breathing. Sin and death are essential parts of the daily, humdrum, dreary way we go along, looking too often to wrong goals, counting on false hopes, believing in spite of ourselves that what little we are able do each day has meaning.

> Naked and alone we came into exile.
> In her dark womb we did not know our mother's face;

from the prison of her flesh we have come into the unspeak-
able and incommunicable prison of this earth.
Which of us has known his brother?
Which of us has looked into his father's heart?
Which of us is not forever a stranger and alone?

Thomas Wolfe's words are words of myth, meaningful
to different times and places to countless people, you and
me, today, yesterday, tomorrow.

Death and sin isolate, causing loneliness and hopeless-
ness, but death and sin make it possible to hear at the Eucharist, and with thanksgiving, the Lord's promise of
truth and righteousness and life.

But before that promise becomes reality, we know the
separateness of sin and death.

I work all day, and get half-drunk at night.
Waking at four to soundless dark, I stare.
In time the curtain edges will grow light.
Till then I see what's really always there:
Unresting death, a whole day nearer now,
Making all thought impossible but how
And where and when I shall myself die.
Arid interrogation: yet the dread
Of dying, and being dead,
Flashes afresh to hold and horrify.

The mind blanks at the glare. Not in remorse
—The good not done, the love not given, time
Torn off unused—nor wretchedly because
An only life can take so long to climb
Clear of its wrong beginnings, and may never;
But at the total emptiness for ever,
The sure extinction that we travel to
And shall be lost in always. Not to be here,
Not to be anywhere,
And soon; nothing more terrible, nothing more true.

                🙰   🙰   🙰

"We give thanks to you, O God, for the goodness and love made known to us in creation...."

Hearing those words, Charles drifted away to remember all those times he had awakened in the middle of the night. No matter how many times this happened—and it had been hundreds of times—he had known in the first instant that he had once again been given life for another day. Always it was early morning, very early, the in-between time, neither dark nor light, before clear sight was possible yet everything terrifyingly clear to his mind's eye. This was a time set apart, everything frighteningly intimate and personal—God's time—the time the hymn writer John Ellerton described when he wrote, "for dark and light are both alike to thee."

Recently, when Nancy had been waking up at the same time, they shared these moments. Experience, memory, hope, dread, fear, joy—all these emotions that they had known and shared were raised up, and new life, new possibility, became immediate and real. Dream and vision, prayer and conversation, reverie and expectation, blended together without distinction—just as their two separate lives did in these moments of dark and light, sleep and reality, two people who were one.

He remembered their talk at this hour. Long bursts of unplanned, random sentences reaching back into childhood and forward into the coming day and beyond to the unknown future. The in-between time brought them freedom to move back into the past and ahead into the future and all directions at once—to know, as one flesh, the fullness of time. The in-between time became the very definition of the word "spiritual": the fullness of life is the journey we undertake through others and with God.

But there were times when he awakened and felt very much alone. Aware of the edge of light just beginning to appear around the window, he knew overwhelming emptiness. What if none of it were true? What if this were all, and the night of death was nothing, absolutely nothing? No one could say this was impossible. The in-between time made that seem real, so real he had to roll over, wrap his arms around Nancy and begin to speak through the darkness to find assurance. He did. To be one flesh with Nancy was to know the promise of truth and righteousness and life. He sensed that the Lord was in this place.

          ﺈﺈ   ﺈﺈ   ﺈﺈ

On the night before he died for us, our Lord Jesus Christ took bread; and when he had given thanks to you, he broke it, and gave it to his disciples, and said, "Take, eat: This is my Body which is given for you. Do this for the remembrance of me."

The bread is broken. He is broken. Nothing continues just as it was, is today, and will be forever unless it comes up against death. "Unless a grain of wheat falls into the earth and dies, it remains alone. But if it dies, it bears much fruit."

Life never remains the same. Either it changes, or it dies. A marriage must grow and evolve into new and deeper patterns of intimacy, or it dies. Friendship of every length and kind deepens and changes, or it will die. No one can undertake the same repetitious and un-changing job day after day without burning out or giving up. New challenges and opportunities must develop from the known and familiar. Any interest or hobby or passion grows and changes, or it dies.

What we often don't realize is that the safe, comfortable, and predictable, the well known and carefully understood, often bring death. Only when the moment comes that we reach our point of no return, it is too late to turn back, too late to live life over again.

John Marquand's novel, *Point of No Return* was a bestselling book and a smash hit as a Broadway play shortly after World War II. Marquand spoke to the dangers of seeking the safe and acceptable, even in a post-war world hungry for certainty. The central character of the novel is an ordinary man who, by dint of effort and brains, manages to do well but always just misses—not quite the right college, the wrong wife, the wrong friends. He never really seems to arrive, but all the time he is getting closer and closer to his life's dream, everyone's dream, the American dream—to be Number One.

Just at this point, he and his wife are invited to dinner by the chief executive. Dinner ends, and the two men retire to the library for brandy and cigars. Suddenly, through the haze of smoke, Charles is told that he is the new vice president, the very one who will eventually succeed to the presidency. Everything he dreamed has come true. But...

> Suddenly [he] felt dull and tired...[The] voice seemed to come from a long way off. There was a weight on [him] again, the same old weight, and it was heavier after that brief moment of freedom. In spite of all those years, in spite of all his striving, it was remarkable how little pleasure he took in final fulfillment. He was Vice President of the Stuyvesant Bank. It was what he had dreamed of long ago, and yet it was not the true texture of early dreams. The whole thing was contrived, an inevitable result, a strangely hollow climax.

The punishment for wanting the wrong thing in life is that you get it.

"Unless a grain of wheat falls into the earth and dies, it remains alone. But if it dies, it bears much fruit." The bread is broken. He is broken. We are broken, aquainted with death so that we may know new life.

After supper he took the cup of wine; and when he had given thanks, he gave it to them, and said, "Drink this, all of you: This is my Blood of the new Covenant, which is shed for you and for many for the forgiveness of sins. Whenever you drink it, do this for the remembrance of me."

> That very day two of them were going to a village named Emmaus, about seven miles from Jerusalem, and talking with each other about all these things that had happened. While they were talking and discussing together, Jesus himself drew near and went with them. But their eyes were kept from recognizing him…So they drew near to the village to which they going. He appeared to be going further, but they constrained him, saying, "Stay with us, for it is toward evening and the day is now far spent." So he went in to stay with them. When he was at table with them, he took the bread and blessed, and broke it, and gave it to them. And their eyes were opened and they recognized him….

St. Luke's story of Jesus's resurrection appearance to his disciples along the road to Emmaus places us as readers and hearers right in the middle of the story. It describes our experience at the Eucharist, the presence of the risen Lord in the breaking of bread and drinking of wine as we come to this table overcome with the grief of death. Our best friend, the close companion on whom we counted for everything, is dead. We come to the Eucharist, our eyes are opened, and here we are met by the risen Lord.

ð   ð   ð

...On a spring day in 1919, after his recovery from the rheumatic fever that had caused him to drop out of M.I.T. with one semester still to complete, he lay on his back working under an automobile in his uncle's garage in Somerville. Battery acid fell into both eyes. Blinded, he never finished M.I.T. nor became an architect. What money remained paid his medical bills. Gillette Safety Razor Company took him on and trained him under their disability program. He changed trolley cars three times on the Boston Elevated each day to reach his work station in South Boston, and in three months became the most efficient quality control worker in the plant, sighted or blind.

He worked for Gillette for twelve years, until he married and his new wife persuaded him to pack up and move with her and her two sons to her house in rural New Hampshire. There was no job and his health was poor. They supported themselves by boarding homeless, retarded adults, supported by state funds. Nothing came their way but the money they earned, $800.00 a year. Each month they sent two dollars to the local parish.

Reading was his constant activity, through Braille and recorded books, when he was not listening to his crystal set or debating politics and baseball with a neighbor. He was informed and alive, constantly talking and thinking little of himself. He reached out of his darkness to say in touch and smile: "There is something precious, worth holding on to. I have held on. I don't ask you to see that or say that, but I ask you to see me, for in my blindness I can see you."

Among my many memories of Warren, each one crystal clear, I see him most vividly standing at the altar rail, unable to kneel, the very last time he and Nellie came into town to a Maundy Thursday Eucharist. Behind his frosted eye glasses, his eyes were open. He did not see me, but he saw the Lord who met him in the Eucharist as Warren took and ate the bread and drank the wine. Warren allowed me to see things to which I had been blind. Most important of all, Warren helped me to see that those who believe in the Lord Jesus and are washed in the blood of the new covenant are bound together forever.

Then he died, and unlike most of us who wear out and give up before our time, Warren never died until the end of his life. His wife wrote, "Yes, Warren believed in Jesus. For over a week he knew that he was going to die and asked me what I was going to do. It was hard to answer, but I did tell him what I planned for his funeral. I told him that I would be lonely but that I expected to see him soon. That seemed to please him."

Therefore, according to his command, O Father,

Celebrant and People

We remember his death,
We proclaim his resurrection,
We await his coming in glory....

In the very midst of the action of the Eucharist all join voices in this affirmation of faith.

Years ago, a friend who never minced words proclaimed to a large group of us: "Don't try to convince me
that the miracles of the New Testament really happened.
If I buy the resurrection, then the miracles are no prob-
lem."

Life lived in the reality of the resurrection is a miracle.
The miracle stories as they appear in the gospels are not
meant to compel belief, but are testaments of the power
of new life. Miracles are a foretaste of the reality of the
resurrection. The resurrection of Jesus Christ is the event
that gives sight to the blind, hearing to the deaf, speech
to the dumb, healing to the sick, new life to the dead. The
resurrection makes all things new.

Throughout our lives death occurs in many different
ways, and the experience of faith is that through death,
there is new life. Just as this happens again and again, so
too shall it be the conclusion of our longest journey. Resurrection is not a one-time event at the end of time—our
time or the world's time. Resurrection is a frequent oc-
currence, not a daily event, but frequent. We welcome it,
but we also dread it. Resurrection is preceeded by death:
bitter, painful, sorrowful and sometimes very slow. Resurrection brings change, the new and unknown, untried
and unexpected. The known, even the deadly known, is
usually more welcome.

Remember once again that after Moses had led his
people out of the bondage of slavery in Egypt into the
freedom of new life in the wilderness, they came close to
rebellion and were in great fear and cried out to the Lord
and said to Moses, "Is it because there are no graves in
Egypt that you have taken us away to die in the wilderness? What have you done to us, in bringing us out of
Egypt? Is not this what we said to you in Egypt, 'Let us

alone and let us serve the Egyptians?' For it would have been better to serve the Egyptians than to die in the wilderness."

Exodus brought new life, and it was not easy. Life that follows resurrection is never the same as the known and the comfortable. It may not be at all welcome. The new is full of challenge and discomfort, but the alternative to eternal life is eternal death. To remain in the same place is to die even while going through all the actions of living.

We must die to become. If we have not known this now, how can we expect to know it on that day when we lie in death and there is prepared for us a dwelling place in the heavens?

         ❧   ❧   ❧

...It was the most difficult thing he had ever done, that he could ever imagine doing. He quit.

The business was a small one, his own creation, his life work. Colleagues, customers, plant, products were all the symbolic extension of his own life, his values. The business flourished. On some days he felt like the conductor of a symphony orchestra; on others he was a parent; sometimes he was a policeman. Life was not perfect, but so what? He was building a world of promise marked by the interchange of many lives that touched and affected each other.

At first he noticed that he was occasionally restless, but he dismissed this and simply found new and more demanding tasks. What was at first occasional became more frequent and increasingly uncomfortable, until finally he felt fear, chilling and pervasive. Something was wrong. He knew what it was, but he couldn't and wouldn't face it. How could he consider giving up his life's work?

For two years he devoted himself to creating a management team, three trusted associates, who knew every aspect of the business, his business. Then he and his wife of thirty years went far away for six months to think, but it didn't help. Nothing really changed. What had embodied his life, been his life for all those years, the business that was his creation, his very own child, no longer defined him or held him. For everything there is a season, and this was the season for a new challenge. They returned home, and he sold the business.

The pain remained, and it increased. Everywhere they looked, there were reminders of past hurts, the threat of growing old in this place where real change had become impossible, where there were no new friends, only former friends who had become aquaintances. Something more had to be done. They decided to put their house on the market and spent some time selecting a new community before moving to the Northwest. Relocated and settled, together they started a new business. Nothing was easy. Each of them had celebrated a fiftieth birthday, and in this new place they were unknown and alone. They comforted one another with the realization that only rose-colored glasses and imperfect hindsight made the past appear better than it really had been.

Time heals and offers new vistas. New life arrived slowly, and brought with it a new kind of hope. This new dwelling place, they realized as they had never done before, was not made with hands. Before long they too would find themselves in a new heaven and a new earth.

If we dwell only on earth, our dwelling place will be a coffin.

                      èa   *èa*   *èa*

> To die—for this into the world you came.
> Yes, to abandon more than you ever conceived as possible:
> All ideas, plans—even the very best and most unselfish—
> hopes and desires,
> All formulas of morality, all reputation for virtue or con-
> sistency or good sense; all cherished theories, doctrines, sys-
> tems of knowledge.
> Modes of life, habits, predilections, preferences, supe-
> riorities, weaknesses, indulgences.
> Good health, wholeness of limb and brain, youth, manhood,
> age—nay life itself—in one word: To die—
> For this into the world you came.
>
> All to be abandoned, and when they have been finally aban-
> doned,
> Then to return to be used—and then only to be rightly used,
> to be free and open forever.

And we offer our sacrifice of praise and thanksgiving to you, O Lord of all; presenting to you, from your creation, this bread and this wine.

The stuff of the Eucharist, the material presented to be used and transformed in this meal of thanksgiving and redemption, is the stuff of our lives. Symbolized in bread and wine, we offer from God's creation materials that embody us, our world, the world made by God, and all that we are and would be in that world. What we offer is perishable. What we receive in turn is imperishable.

Ernest Becker's book, *The Denial of Death*, written only shortly before his own death, asserts that each of us devotes the major part of our energy avoiding the central reality of life: death. His insight is summed up in this contemporary parable.

æ   æ   æ

...Feeding time at the zoo, and into the python cage the keeper casts three plump and vigorous chickens. Their noise and activity wakens the hungry and sleeping giant reptile in the far corner, and as the chickens quietly devote themselves to pecking at the corn in the near corner, the snake uncoils and plans his approach and attack, slithering through the straw, until with one motion he captures and devours the chicken nearest to him.

As we watch the bird disappear, and the quivering lump slowly quiet as it advances down the snake's alimentary canal, the other two birds go berserk. White feathers fly everywhere, as they flap against the bars and squawk and scream. In time the noise lessens. The python returns to his corner, coils and sleeps, and the chickens return to pecking, unaware that in time the snake will wake and take them, one at a time. Death waits in the corner. For now, they peck.

æ   æ   æ

So do we. Anything is better than thinking about the death that awaits us. Our perishable lives here we offer in the Eucharist, knowing that we must die to become. We know this now, but we shall know it more fully in that day when our mortal body lies in death, and there is prepared for us a dwelling place eternal in the heavens.

133

We pray you, gracious God, to send your Holy Spirit upon these gifts that they may be the Sacrament of the Body of Christ and his Blood of the new Covenant. Unite us to your Son in his sacrifice, that we may be acceptable through him, being sanctified by the Holy Spirit. In the fullness of time, put all things in subjection under your Christ, and bring us to that heavenly country where with all your saints, we may enter the everlasting heritage of your sons and daughters; through Jesus Christ our Lord, the first born of all creation, the head of the Church and the author of our salvation.

By him, and with him, and in him, in the unity of the Holy Spirit all honor and glory is yours, Almighty Father, now and for ever. Amen.

That heavenly country will be our abiding place only through Jesus Christ our Lord. We may dislike and try to avoid dependency, clinging, in all the forms it takes, but finally we are all dependent on the grace of God that is ours through Jesus Christ. The words of many prayers that conclude over and over again with the words "through Jesus Christ our Lord" are the foretaste of what awaits us in that name and presence in the heavenly country. In that country he has prepared a place for us; there we go to join him, and all the saints, who are joined with all his sons and daughters, every person—known and unknown, remembered and forgotten—who has gone before us through Jesus Christ our Lord.

We meet them now in prayer. We meet them here in this celebration of bread and wine, death and new life. So then, we shall meet them face to face.

THE POST COMMUNION COLLECT
As the Eucharist ends, we kneel to offer thanks.

Almighty God, we thank you that in your great love you have fed us with the spiritual food and drink of the Body and Blood of your Son Jesus Christ, and have given us a foretaste of your heavenly banquet. Grant that this Sacrament may be to us a comfort in affliction, and a pledge of our inheritance in that kingdom where there is no death, neither sorrow now crying, but the fullness of joy with all your saints; through Jesus Christ our Savior. Amen.

The Book of Common Prayer understands and proclaims the Christian faith at table. The central act is a meal, eating and drinking, bread and wine. The practice originates in the Passover Seder, the gathering of family and friends to rehearse the drama of salvation. The meal is related to all our ordinary meals, all the times when family and friends sit together in one place and time to share sustenence and self. The symbolism of feeding and refreshment is unavoidable—the opportunity to pause, reflect, give thanks, gather strength.

Each of us has a history that includes the memory of shared meals. The act of giving thanks through bread and wine are the roots of the Eucharist. Food eaten in thanksgiving, for sustenance, and in the midst of our dailyness assumes a central place and directs us towards the heavenly banquet.

The evening meals of my childhood took place around the family dinner table, a gathering in a familiar place and at an appointed time to tell, to learn, and to weave the fabric of the family. These were blended into the singular act of sharing a meal and created memories that

135

still sustain me. Conversation centered on family history, literature, language, the gathering together of the events of the day, and thoughts of the future. These moments still stand out, decades later, as times of intimacy and learning. They were made possible by the act of sharing a meal.

The setting was important. Always there was candlelight, proclaiming that dinner was the event of the day. My seat was defined by the mirror on the wall behind me and the clock opposite me. My parents were always there. Our exact conversations are not important. There was a tone and spirit, a series of moments that taught me the importance of reading and writing, history and tradition, the necessity of devoting what there was of my life to what I believed and what I could profess.

The facts learned around that dinner table may have been irrelevant, although I doubt that I shall ever believe it unimportant that "none" takes a singular verb; the principles taught there embodied and defined our family. These are timeless. They include the belief that while we should always support each other in our decisions, each of us makes those decisions alone. Decisions reflect what you profess, what you believe. What you do with your lifetime is your profession. We are known to ourselves, to others and to God by our fruits, which is to say, what we do with our life, our single and most precious gift.

Don't ask me how I know that. I just do. Don't you? What else could be so clear? This was what I heard and discussed as we ate meat and potatoes, and broke bread together.

Slowly it dawned on me that learning is not merely the exchange of information, but the rooting of experience in family and community when we gather for nourishment. This is what happens in the eucharistic meal.

And so when the funeral is over, and everyone has eaten the bread and wine of the Eucharist, they come together again afterwards to eat and drink and tell stories, and remember the friend who is dead and has been gathered into the company of saints. "Jesus said to them, 'I am the bread of life; he who comes to me shall not hunger, and he who believes in me shall never thirst.'"

No two things are more important for children as they grow up in a family than eating together and reading together. Parents of high school age children no longer read aloud to their children—did they ever? The place of reading—reading shared, books exchanged and discussed—remains. The proper place for that kind of exchange, every kind of daily exchange, is the family dinner table. Otherwise there will be no family, no learning, no memory, no common history, no future.

As these two essential family pastimes threaten to be replaced totally by television and fast food outlets, no family life will remain. When we lose the table, we lose too the altar as our central symbol and all it proclaims and foretells.

The family dinner table is none other than the "foretaste of your heavenly banquet." There is not to be some moment when everything changes beyond recognition. Yes, there are endings, and there are beginnings—but each follows the other. The banquet begins at home and continues at the altar rail.

ðŸ™ƒ   ðŸ™ƒ   ðŸ™ƒ

As we moved from pew to altar rail to receive the bread and wine, we sang.

> The peace of God, it is no peace,
> But strife closed in the sod.
> Yet let us pray for but one thing—
> The marvelous peace of God.

The wafer was in my hand. "The Body of Christ. The Bread of Heaven." She was next to me. I burst into tears, overwhelmed by the full weight of the past, those left behind, the unclaimed and the unknown, hope for the future, and yes, the love that surrounded us at this table. Even in this strange and scary place, somehow, in some way, the love and peace of Christ existed.

> Think not that your world will change.
> What you know now
> Is what you will know then.

This is more than a foretaste, but the beginning of the very end of our longest journey. The Eucharist, this sacrament of bread and wine, is a pledge of what the future brings, that time of the kingdom where life as we know it will be redeemed and changed.

❧　　❧　　❧

...The funeral in the state mental hospital began as a friend of the dead patient played "Rock of Ages" on his harmonica.

The place smelled of indifference, and certain areas reminded him more of the monkey house at the zoo than anywhere else he had ever been. Every window was bare, covered on the outside with heavy iron mesh. The walls, dirty and scarred, had last been painted a pale green in the late 1960s. Mismatched furniture collected from different garage sales, battered and ripped, was scattered here and there. High ceilings cast everywhere a cold, bright light. When the small ragged band of friends gathered in the corner of the day room to pay their last respects, the first chords of "Rock of Ages" went through him like an electric shock, bringing warmth and memories, where everything else was cold and unfamiliar.

The rag-tag band, off key and out of time, seemed as closely bound together as his large extended family that once gathered around grandfather's table on Thanksgiving Day and sang, "We Gather Together." For reasons he had forgotten, he knew that this group too was gathered in the name of one unknown and forgotten. When the Lord had come, he came to such as these, the lost and neglected, the poor and the sick.

One old woman sat back on an upholstered chair in the corner, her grey cotton dress caught just above her stretch elastic support hose. Her friend stood by in a plaid shirt butttoned to the neck, brown suspenders hoisting up corduroy pants; he kept opening and closing his mouth to reveal widely scattered teeth. A younger woman rocked back and forth in time with the music, as they listened to the old harmonica and sang.

He knew that if God were anywhere, He was right here in this dreary, God-forsaken place. This was God's place—forgotten, misused, dirty, understaffed. If time had stood still, then they all together, at one time and in one place, might have known more than they could ever let on, more than they had ever known before.

When he completed the blessing, the harmonica player drew out every last chord of "Taps." After the final note, dead silence. No one moved.

ॐ   ॐ   ॐ

The foretaste of the kingdom is found in different times and places, most of them unexpected.

> Several years ago George and I
> Went fishing through the ice on Round Pond.
> We found only three or four inches of ice,
> Enough to hold us and set our rigs,
> Though every now and then it cracked and groaned
> And settled just a bit to frighten us.
> But someone had already tried the pond,
> Some two, I mean, and not been there to fish.
> They'd risked some skating there on quite thin ice,
> A boy and girl, I think, from what they wrote.
> They left their story etched upon the ice.
> They started off together hand in hand,
> Two souls and bodies making now as one—
> Facing the moon over the dark pines,
> Lighting up the great granite cliffs,
> Sparkling on the waters of the brook
> Flowing out to bigger ponds and streams
> And still unfrozen, murmuring in the dark.
> You may, I suppose, think what you will of them.
> I think that they were just a boy and girl
> Not so young as to be vain and silly,
> Old enough for life, moonlight and dark.
> They traced all 'round the edges of the pond,
> And then walked slowly up the slope again,
> Returning to familiar roads and ways.
> Their venture in the dark is something they
> Will cherish all their lives, and I all mine.

We find a taste of the kingdom where we will. A former teacher of mine, a little-known poet, farmer, saint, and theologian realized the promise of God and the mark of heaven in this simple event of two lovers skating on black ice. The kingdom is available to those who have eyes to see and ears to hear. "You may, I suppose, think what you will...."

One clear option is to cherish what one has seen and heard both in this life and for the next.

❧   ❧   ❧

...July 30th. They hadn't seen each other in months and today they met in the worst heat of midsummer. She suggested a restaurant located in the basement of what once had been a garage in Harvard Square. On this unusually hot and humid day the air conditioning was loud and not very effective. He began to sweat. What were they going to talk about? For as well as they had come to know one another, still they were not completely comfortable with each other, especially when sitting face to face across the awkwardly high, crude and narrow restaurant table for two made of rough pine.

He ordered a pizza and then wished he hadn't. She made a big show of getting up and going to the salad bar, poking endlessly through the different kinds of greens, the cucumbers, the olives, the unripe tomatoes. He sat and watched her.

When she came back his pizza had arrived, the one he didn't want. She looked at the pizza and then at him.

"Are you one of those clergymen who prays out loud in restaurants?"

He looked indignant and then they both began to laugh with relief. They could talk now, and they did, far too much, interrupting each other, sharing the salad bar and the pizza, and as they ate and talked, the one who brought life from death was in their midst.

141

CHAPTER VI

A Sinner of Your Own Redeeming

The Commmendation

IS BODY TREMBLED. "I love you," he said out loud. Charles looked around. He thought he heard a reply. He had not slept well, all alone in their bed, missing Nancy again and again, every time he rolled over and reached across the empty space and discovered she was gone. But he had not lost his mind. Nancy was dead. Her body lay in the casket in the aisle, two feet from where he sat, but nevertheless he had heard her reassure him of her love.

He heard her again and sat up, staring straight ahead at the altar and the cross hanging over it. Death was a fact. Death was *the* fact. The cross proclaimed it.

The two arms of the cross were surrounded by a circle, unending, proclaiming eternity. Death is inevitable: the first fact. But just as inevitable as death is eternal life through Jesus Christ who died on that cross. Death first. Then life through death. What eternal life could mean for the two of them, Nancy and Charles, right now, overwhelmed him.

Whatever had been—the years of their life together, good times and bad—this could never be taken away from him. He could summon at will every detail of their life together. Every moment they had shared still belonged to him, unchanged by death. It belonged to Nancy, too, whose presence was close and very real. What he had heard her say did not come from his imagination. The power of their love remained strong. The cross hanging before him made clear what he had come to know in their life together. What he had known then, he still knew now.

He had not always known it. They had both learned it through years of trial and error, struggle and pain, anger and joy. At one time or another he had questioned, and they both had doubted, doubted everything, but not now. Now there was pain and the hollowness of Nancy's absence. He was angry that she had left, but the anger was hollow, and that hollowness surrounded him and embraced him. Nothing could ever make it go away, nothing between now and the grave, but at the same time she was right here.

Love was not immortal. Nancy was not immortal. Nothing was immortal, except for God. But love is eternal, and it went from strength to strength, even through death. He spoke aloud, "I love you."

        ૐ   ૐ   ૐ

The Burial of the Dead concludes here within the church with the Commendation. Before any words are spoken, the ministers *take their places at the body.* The congregation is gathered about the body as the body of the church, emphasizing the reality that in death, as in life, we are gathered together as a community. Death happens to each of us individually, but we are never alone, whether in life or in grief or in death.

The words of the Commendation open with an anthem, repeated twice, echoing familiar themes that look forward through death and beyond time.

Give rest, O Christ, to your servant with your saints,
where sorrow and pain are no more,
neither sighing, but life everlasting.

          ❧   ❧   ❧

..."There are no marriages in heaven. There are no marriages in heaven. There are no marriages in heaven." Over and over again she heard the words repeated.

It was not clear who spoke or how she heard or even where she was. There had been a great sense of peace and well-being, and then floating before her, those words. She sensed all kinds of activity around the bed, but none of it mattered. The light was all that mattered, and the sense of peace and the words, "There are no marriages in heaven."

She listened more intently. The voice was one of authority. Her mother? No, it belonged to Father Hardman. The rector had been a constant in her childhood. His words had affected her long before her marriage. Father Hardman had officiated at their wedding, but only after long conversations about marriage in his study. Once he had said to them, "There are no marriages in heaven. But remember that from the moment you come before God's altar until you are parted by death, you belong to one another and only to one another. Never forget that. God bless you."

In spite of those days when she could have killed Frank if only someone had handed her the knife, the years of their marriage had been more than she had dreamed. Of course he could be difficult, stubborn, hardly perfect, but so often gracious, able see the light, to offer compromise. The give and take was real, and she loved him from that very first day he had walked up onto her parents' front porch until the awful night when he rose from the table and collapsed, right in the middle of dinner. He was sixty-three. That was years ago. It seemed she missed him now even more. Every day she missed him and felt his presence.

The grief had been unbearable at first. Gradually she had learned to live with it, and despite what Father Hardman had said, she knew she and Frank were still married.

"There are no marriages in heaven," she heard the words again, and their spell ended. The bright white light continued to blind her, then gradually faded. She found herself on her parents' front porch once again. The screen door swung open.

≥   ≥   ≥

The story may be a fantasy, but it is a fantasy that many of us share. Time will tell. Life ends, marriage ends, every human undertaking and construction ends. That is reality. But there is more. The First Letter of John states: "God is love, and he who abides in love abides in God, and God abides in him."

And now we pray.

You only are immortal, the creator and maker of mankind; and we are mortal, formed of the earth, and to earth we shall return. For so did you ordain when you created me, saying, "You are dust, and to dust you shall return." All of us go down to the dust; yet even at the grave we make our song: Alleluia, alleluia, alleluia.

...Shortly after his graduation from high school, a former student wrote a letter to his faculty advisor.

"Leaving school after commencement was encountering death. Graduation is final. I will never return as the person I am now, only as a graduate. I don't belong there anymore. My home for several years has been taken away, forever, and I will always know that regret.

"But if there is one thing I have learned from this and other deaths, it is the part that death plays. Too many people spend their years refusing to realize that death enters all our lives. Death is part of life, a part that enriches. We shouldn't squander time worrying over trivial matters such as getting up the corporate ladder. The time we have on this earth is all the time we have, something I am just beginning to learn. I thank God for this learning, the most important of my life."

❧   ❧   ❧

"Finishing my first book was a kind of death. Before, I would...."

He had been talking vigorously with his editor for several minutes, talking about his book. Then, recalling the moment he had first known he was finished, the very last page rewritten, the last page for the very last time, he stopped in mid-sentence and pretended to look away,

147

knowing she was watching. The two had worked together closely, and the book had become an integral part of his life. Now it was finished, there was nothing more to be done. Soon it would be published and have a life of its own, and it no longer belonged to him.

Something new had been created. Now it lay there, on the table between them. One of them had to lean over and pick it up and discover how there could be new life after the old had ended.

ò&   ò&   ò&

...After three years of marriage, the death of two parents, and extended separations, they decided that the time had come for children. Only it didn't happen, and it continued not to happen after each had undergone every kind of test. Nothing, absolutely nothing, was wrong, but still no conception, nothing grew except their pain and the realization that they would never have one of the essential experiences of being an adult: parenthood.

For long periods of time they said nothing to each other. She began to inquire into the requirements for foster parenthood and adoption. He had another fertility test and still her period came as regular as the cycles of the moon, month by month. The pain escalated, never departing from them, whether separate or together. The barrier between them grew, threatening to engulf and destroy them. At last nothing remained but to confront the monster, to welcome it, kiss it, bless it.

The conversation came at dinner on a cold Tuesday evening in February.

"I went to see Dr. Murphy today. He told me there was no point in coming back again, not for a year at least."

"How come?"

"Because apparently we're not going to have a child. That's how come. And unless I'm going to get pregnant, there's no point in going to see the obstetrician."

A long silence, and finally, he asked, "Now what?"

"I left his office and went around the corner to begin the adoption process."

"We've talked about that before. The only child to live in this house will be ours. That's not much to ask."

"But it's not going to happen. Come on, face it. We've got to face it. We are never, never, never, never going to have a child."

They both began to weep, still sitting at opposite ends of the table. Neither moved, but neither turned away. They would never be parents. Life would go on, but the dreams of their courtship, dreams of their later years surrounded by a growing family, these dreams were dead.

Once the words were spoken and the acknowledgement clear, they went about their business with new freedom. She ovulated next on the tenth of March, and, on that very night, as if by a miracle, their first daughter was conceived. They named her Sarah in memory of the once-barren mother of a long race of chosen people.

Give rest, O Christ, to your servant with your saints,
where sorrow and pain are no more,
neither sighing, but life everlasting.

ෙ෧   ෙ෧   ෙ෧

Before departure from the church building, in procession, the body is blessed.

Into your hands, O merciful Savior, we commend your servant N. Acknowledge, we humbly beseech you, a sheep of your own fold, a lamb of your own flock, a sinner of your own redeeming. Receive her into the arms of your mercy, into the blessed rest of everlasting peace, and into the glorious company of the saints in light. Amen.

Sheep...Lamb...Sinner. The images all hinge on our belonging both to Christ and to one another. At no time, living or dead, are we alone, isolated, separated, but a member of the body—at one.

Personal reminiscences after a death are apt to idealize and even canonize the departed. The burial service has no such illusions. We are reminded that sin holds us all captive, even this one, whom we may have loved more than life itself. Still, even as we are held by sin, we are also held in the loving arms of the Christ, to whom we belong and who redeems us all.

          ❧   ❧   ❧

..."Do you believe that the good can choose the hour of their death?" asked the doctor as he picked up the empty pill bottle, sitting next to her bed. The two men had entered the guest room together after the doctor had arrived, six hours later than expected, to certify grandmother's death.

No one knew when or how it had happened, only that the fifteen-year-old granddaughter had heard no response at 9:30 when she finally knocked on the door to deliver fresh orange juice. It was late for Nana to be waking, but then she had been under an unusual strain since Baba had died in the middle of his bath three weeks ago. Disconnected and disenfranchised, Nana had spent most of those twenty-odd days wandering aimlessly through the world she once had known, now destroyed by her husband's death.

The day before had been joyous, Christmas. Her family had gathered around her. She had returned from the mists and joined them, once again, to be part of the family. The day ended. She mounted the stairs slowly, and the children tucked her into bed. Kisses all around, and they sneaked out of her room and down the hall, even as she began to fall asleep. Next to her bed on the night table, the familiar glass, a pitcher of water, and the pills.

Had she fallen to sleep right then? Or had she waited for the silence and then snapped on the light and opened the bottle? No one really knew but God, the same God who long ago named her good and had chosen the hour of her death.

            ই   ই   ই

...The pregnancy was normal, but the day the boy was born, his father knew something was not quite right. The next day, they were told that the child had Downs Syndrome.

For a month, each night in bed they clung to each other, mother and father, and cried and cried. There was nothing else to do. Finally, very late one night, after each had dropped off to sleep, he wakened, rose, and walked automatically into the nursery. He leaned over the crib and their sleeping baby, laid his hands on his son's head, and said, "Lord. You know I want this boy healed. Make him whole."

151

Through the years that followed, he often told what had happened then. "The room was filled with warmth. That's what it felt like. And from somewhere inside me a voice said, 'John, everything's going to be all right.'"

Years later the boy was accepted into the tenth grade of the city high school, became the manager of the championship football team, received a gold medal for the hundred-yard dash in the Special Olympics, and on graduation, dressed in cap and gown, received his special diploma in an auditorium where every person stood and cheered. He went off to work on his own, lived with another mentally handicapped person, was more than once promoted in his job, and found his life constantly renewed and rewarded.

He wasn't "normal," but he was whole. Everything was all right.

ᨖ   ᨖ   ᨖ

Each of us is a sheep of his own fold, a lamb of his own flock, a sinner of his own redeeming.

Each of us sees the world, the same world, from a different perspective. No one else knows what it is like to live inside my skin. How can they? That is a heavy burden, one we all carry. Death releases us from that burden to new life. Death also releases those who mourn to see the burden for what it is. It is a burden we all share, a burden that can be taken from us through the love and life and death of God, who has redeemed us all. Through our own death, through our own mourning for the death of another, again, we are joined to the very death of God. There is release, and there is new life.

Each of us lives and dies a sinner, a person caught within a web, the prisoner of our perception that the world is only as I see it. Such a view is too narrow, a misperception, false.

The world is as God sees it. God created it. God lived in it. God redeemed it. We belong to God in life and in death and in all life to come.

Therefore, we say as we turn to leave this service:

Let us go forth in the name of Christ.
Thanks be to God.

The body is borne from the church. We rise and follow, marking time to these anthems of departure, words of victory.

Christ is risen from the dead, trampling down death by death, and giving life to those in the tomb.

When Christians proclaim incarnation—the fact that God revealed himself in human flesh as Jesus Christ—we mean that God was part of all human life, every single part of our experience. Such experience includes death. God in Christ lived with us. God in Christ died with us. God in Christ overcame death.

Whenever we encounter death, defeat, or loss, we seek first the one who has already been there. The first person each of us wants when hurt is someone who has been hurt in just the same way. The alcoholic is drawn to Alcoholics Anonymous. The person recently divorced does not rush home to celebrate a sister's twenty-fifth wedding anniversary, but would rather be with someone who has known the recent and painful death of a marriage.

Just after failing the bar exam, I am not about to be found on the doorstep of my Phi Beta Kappa college roommate. And when we have been fired, we seek first and only the company of the friend who has also known such failure. There is new and unknown strength in being bound to another who knows what it means to be wounded, just as I have been wounded.

Jesus is that person.

The Sun of Righteousness is gloriously risen, giving light to those who sit in darkness and in the shadow of death.

When we sit in darkness and in the shadow of death, we want to sit with one who is aquainted with that darkness, our darkness. No one else will do. Not right then.

      ੴ   ੴ   ੴ

...The boy was still young, fourteen, slightly older than his sister. Life at home was in great disarray. His father, a surgeon, was seldom there, always out for dinner and gone the first thing every morning. Whenever the family was together, there was nothing but anger and fighting.

The son had taken about all he could. Nothing seemed to help; there was no one to talk to. At first he put everything into his school work, then he just gave up and did nothing, spent time alone, avoided everyone and everything.

The parents decided finally to put an end to their bad marriage after using the help of every kind of counselor, none of whom was helpful. Father moved in with the scrub nurse, who had been occupying all of his time, and mother was left alone, for good and all, with the kids.

Someone still had to deal with the boy. On good advice and after careful thought, she chose the school guidance counselor. After all, the counselor was older, a parent with children of the same age, happily married, secure, compassionate. He agreed to offer the helping and understanding hand, and the appointment was set for ten o'clock next Thursday.

The boy was late, hanging back deliberately outside the office door until the man came to fetch him. Never raising his head, he entered the room, slouched down on the couch and pretended to study the pattern on the tile floor.

"Jamie," the counselor began, "you've been through a bad patch. Things are tough at home, real tough. I know that. Well, I just wanted you to come by and have a little chat with me. You see, I understand what's going on in your life. I understand, and I don't want you to feel so alone."

He paused. Jamie said nothing. He tried again.

"Jamie. There are a lot of people here who care about you. I'm one of them. We want you to know that you can reach out to us. We'll help. We'll understand. You're having a tough time with all that's going on with your mother and dad, I know. But you're not alone. Can you understand?"

He paused again. Again, silence. He let the silence hang there in the air between them. It lasted for what seemed like a long time.

Without raising his head nor removing his hands from either side of his face, Jamie asked, "Are you finished?"

"Yes."

"Then may I go now?"

"Yes."

The boy rose and in one motion turned and left the room in silence.

❧ ❧ ❧

When we sit in darkness and in the shadow of death, there are many people who have no knowledge of what that means. We want to sit with one who knows what it means to be in our kind of darkness, one who will lighten that darkness with a special understanding. Jesus is that person.

The Lord will guide our feet into the way of peace, having taken away the sin of the world.

He guides our feet into the way of peace with a presence that is first at one with us, but then apart from us; by Him we are made whole enough to live anew.

❧ ❧ ❧

...As he sat in the hospital waiting room, he had no clear memory of how he had gotten there. It had all happened so suddenly. Her pain, the call for help, the arrival of the ambulance, the emergency room. Then she was whisked away, and he was dispatched to this cold and sterile place. It was midnight, and not another living person in sight.

Without thinking he rose, fished some change from his pocket, walked over to the telephone book under the pay phone on the wall, looked up a number, and dialed. It rang twice. A voice answered. Incoherently, he told his story.

"I don't know what to do. It's Sarah. Emergency Room. Can you help me? I don't know what's going on."

Fifteen minutes later, his friend appeared in the room, sat down next to him, and remained through the night.

Sixteen years passed. Just blocks from where they had sat on that long night a farewell gathering took place to honor the retirement of the friend who had come to sit with him. Speeches, words of thanks, laughter and tears, and many grateful friends. He waited for his moment when the guest of honor would be free.

"Remember the night when I called from the Emergency Room, and you came and sat up with me while Sarah had surgery?"

"Yes, Tom, I remember."

"Well, I've never forgotten that. Here's a token." He pressed into the hand of his friend a small package. "Thank you."

"Thank you, Tom. But you know, I don't remember one single thing I said that night."

"You never said a word. You sat there with me."

&a.   &a.   &a.

Surely on this earth, not only must God's work be our own, but Jesus wears many faces, possesses many feet and hands and ears and eyes. He comes to us. We too must go to others in his name and presence; otherwise, neither we nor they will be made whole to live anew.

Christ will open the kingdom of heaven to all who believe in his Name, saying, Come, O blessed of my Father; inherit the kingdom prepared for you.

This anthem evokes Jesus' story of the last judgment and our appearance before the King to testify on our own behalf. At that day the King will say to those on his right hand, "Come, O blessed of my Father, inherit the kingdom prepared for you from the foundation of the world; for I was hungry and you gave me food, I was thirsty and you gave me drink, I was a stranger and you welcomed me, I was naked and you clothed me, I was sick and you visited me, I was in prison and you came to me."

Each of us is a sinner. It is Christ who died to save us from our own narrowness and pettiness and willingness to think of self before the needs of our neighbor. This anthem reminds us, who are at the very gates of death, that the prison in which we live is of our own making. It is our choice, and our choice alone, to open the doors that hold us captive and reach out beyond those doors to the others who cross our path. Those others are there in His name and image. When we find and are found by them, we find the Lord, and we find new life that releases us from sin and death.

ﺰ&   ﺰ&   ﺰ&

...The waiting room of LaSalle Street Station in Chicago was crowded, and the train was late. He and his wife sat on their suitcases and watched the people and waited to board the Empire Builder. Among the several hundred people, the wealthier waited for Pullman accommodations and stood out in their custom-made suits and hand-made shoes. Far more were rumpled, nondescript, and appeared tired, while in a far corner an old woman, feet bound in rags, rummaged through a trash can.

Too many people for him. The station felt so strange and oppressive. More and more uncomfortable every minute, he searched for a way to set himself apart, above the crowd as it milled around him. He began to mock and belittle, to remove the threat that surrounded him— so many people who were so different.

He began to talk to his wife, to ramble, to ridicule. Beginning with bad Polish jokes, he went from there to comments, insults that slipped out far too easily, sarcasm. He attacked the dress, hygiene, speech and intelligence of everyone around him. Everything he said made him feel more and more isolated and alone.

Throughout her husband's monologue she made no response. Finally he seemed to have finished, calling a man in a wheel chair nearby a "cripple." Then she turned, looked him full in the face, and said:

"Christ died for that man. Christ died for every single person in this station."

The Station Master announced that the Empire Builder was ready to receive passengers on Track Number Six.

ৼ   ৼ   ৼ

Christ comes to us in those for whom he died. So too we go in His name wherever and whenever we are. "And whoever gives to one of these little ones even a cup of cold water because he is a disciple, truly, I say to you, shall not lose his reward."

Into paradise may the angels lead you. At your coming may the martyrs receive you, and bring you into the holy city Jerusalem.

159

Jerusalem, "the city of peace," is the symbol of unity and home and heaven. It is everything for which we hope, the great end and real business of our common life. Our image of Jerusalem includes our every under-standing of homecoming and family and holiday.

> Then I saw a new heaven and a new earth; for the
> first heaven and the first earth had passed away,
> and the sea was no more. And I saw the holy city,
> new Jerusalem, coming down out of heaven from
> God, prepared as a bride adorned for her husband;
> and I heard a great voice from beyond the throne
> saying, "Behold the dwelling place of God is with
> men. He will dwell with them, and they shall be
> his people, and God himself will be with them; he
> will wipe away every tear from their eyes, and
> death shall be no more, neither shall there be
> mourning nor crying nor pain any more, for the
> former things have passed away."

ﺰ   ﺰ   ﺰ

...The three-year-old child developed a brain tumor and after treatment went into remission for five years. Then the tumor reappeared. After the child died, her mother said, "The worst part of all was that I couldn't love her enough. I could never give myself to her because I knew I would lose her."

But it was more than that. She found that one by one she could not maintain even her oldest and best friend-ships. Everyone, even old and good friends, seemed so flat, so frivolous. She told herself again and again that since nothing lasted in this world, how could a few fool-ish friends possibly matter? What was the point? Every-thing came to an end, so why bother? She couldn't and didn't.

Their daughter died three days before her ninth birthday. The following winter she and Sam decided to separate after fifteen years of marriage. Their years had been good ones despite the pain, but now a thick barrier stood between them. They knew why it was there, but it wouldn't budge and neither would they.

Everywhere she turned, she saw her daughter's face. The way she had smiled up at her from her bassinet, banged her cup on the high chair, hugged her teddy bear, rode her tricycle, turned back to wave as she ran for the schoolbus. She remembered particularly one day last fall, leaves blowing, the smell of rain in the air, when she had watched her step down from the school bus and run towards the car. She dropped her red sweater, turned back, picked it up, and ran again towards her mother. The memory remained. The child was hers, suspended in time. Nothing could take that away.

Where was her daughter now? Probably she was nowhere at all, despite the well-meaning friends who said she was with God. She wanted to believe that, but it seemed hollow and mysterious. Every night when she slept her little girl was so alive in her dreams. When she awoke, the memories continued throughout the day. She wished she could have loved her more when she was alive and not allowed the distance, for now her little girl, her precious daughter, was so close.

 махмахмах

...In the early stages of his illness making love provided a partial relief from her despair, but that was finished now. She was becoming afraid of her own body, afraid of its demands, afraid to look at other men, especially when she caught them looking at her. They often did. She was still very attractive and he was the one who had leukemia. Just how far did that old business of "in sickness and health" go? As far as she was concerned, right now was just about far enough. If he was going to die, why didn't he go ahead and get it over with?

Whenever she talked like that to herself, she felt dirty. What was she, nothing but a bitch in heat that craved mating? It was men who carried their brains in their balls. She was of a different order, a person set apart for finer things. Did this mean she was different from him? He could barely raise his head from the pillow.

She looked at him, lying so still, as if asleep. God, how she loved him. But goddamn it, was just loving him enough? She needed to prove it, prove it with her body. Could they ever make love again, the way they once had, young and sweet and first in love, and not sick, not sick, not sick.

æ   æ   æ

...I opened my friend's bathroom cabinet one evening, looking for some aspirin, and came across a large cache of red and yellow sleeping pills, fifty at least. I walked back downstairs and said, "I'm not going home until you tell me what you're doing with that stash of pills upstairs." All the color drained from his face, and he turned and walked from the room, pretending he had not heard me.

The evening dragged on interminably, and it was well after midnight before the first few guests began to collect their coats and disappear. Camped out in my chair in the corner, I remained until the last guest had gone home.

When he returned to the living room, expecting to find it empty, he was startled to see me still sitting there. "I'm not going home until you tell me what you're doing with that stash of pills upstairs."

"I need them to sleep. I have trouble getting to sleep."

"Sleep! You've got enough for an army to sleep. That's a lie, and you know it! What are they for?"

"They're for just in case."

Silence.

"Just in case of what."

He shook his head, looking confused. "I'm not sure. In case something happens."

"I'm sorry. I wish I'd known about your pain. Has it been that bad?"

We were both silent for a very long time. He said, "It's been awful, just awful. I'm so lonely. I want somebody to care about me. I can't sleep or eat. I've lost seventeen pounds, mostly in the last two months. I didn't need that. I don't need any of this."

The silence was far longer this time, but we both waited. It was my turn. "Please forgive me for minding your business, but your business is my business. I've been there, where you are right now. Maybe tonight I'll be there again. No one else in the world may know what it is like for you, but I think I know. That may not change it for you one bit, except it means you can throw those pills away."

≈   ≈   ≈

The service had ended. Charles and the family hunched together in the rain as they walked from the church, and wordlessly slid into two different cars to drive to the cemetery.

CHAPTER VII

The Blood of the Everlasting Covenant

The Committal

C HARLES STOOD BY THE grave. The sky had clouded over while they were in church and now it was beginning to rain. He could reach out and touch the casket, look down into the square hole, dark and concrete-lined, hold hands with the children. What would Nancy think of this?

Sometimes when she became angry, she had made a list of the men she wanted as pall bearers, beginning with the little boy who sat in front of her in first grade and the two high school sweethearts. The list included Henry, to whom she had been engaged briefly at the age of twenty, and concluded with several of Charles's friends whom she found interesting and attractive. Charles did not make the list. "Don't bother to come," she would say. "It might spoil your day. We wouldn't want that!"

Each time, after the list was complete, she would ask his advice, simply to enrage him, and when he began to boil, she would add, "This will be the first day of the rest of your life, while my *good* friends are burying me. Shall we plan for your time alone? Will there be a new friend?

Someone to enjoy the way you forget the names of all her good friends and drink too much and never remember birthdays or anniversaries. I can just picture her, can't you?"

She hadn't been completely serious, or so it seemed now. It hadn't been very funny, and usually ended in a fight, but the memory still made him smile. So like Nancy—she was always different, never run-of-the-mill. Not someone who would go and get herself hit by a truck and abandon him. That was too mundane, it wasn't like her. She had to be still around somewhere, but where?

Everyone the Father gives to me will come to me;
I will never turn away anyone who believes in me.

The priest's opening words at graveside tell us where the person we have come to mourn is to be found—with Jesus. This is what the words say. This is what we believe. This is why we are here.

...Afterwards, months after she died, it seemed to him that he could follow her lead, not by dying, but by changing. It was as if her death had been a venture into the unforeseen and the new.

The very idea made him feel uncomfortable, disloyal. After all, theirs had been a remarkable marriage—bound, almost rooted, one to the other. Sex was passionate,

166

physical but also much more. When he was inside her, he was truly inside, one flesh, until parted by death.

Now death had done just that. Where now was the spirit they had known in their love. Was it gone forever? He refused to believe that. Death, especially her death, had to be an adventure. Just as he saw her no more, so now her whole being was involved in an exploration of the unseen. The world they had known together, all that had become blessed, familiar, sacred, was gone. What had taken its place was the call to the new, the unknown that lay beyond: a new dimension.

Once they had not been. He had not been. She had not been. Then they happened. Each one had come to be, together, a new thing. No more. That was over. Now she was dead. The horizon beckoned to what lay beyond: the unseen and new.

She had died, and he had been alone and lost. Every bearing and boundary gone, he staggered in space, weightless. Time passed, and he came to know that even though she was gone, she had not ceased to be. The days of her life had been a constant testimony to the power of renewal, new life, the ability to be born again in surprising ways, always unpredictable. If this was the way it always had been, he thought, that is how it would continue, for her and for him.

He who raised Jesus Christ from the dead
will also give new life to our mortal bodies
through his indwelling spirit.

The Christian truth of death and resurrection, proclaimed and embodied in Jesus, reaches out to touch us. Theories of death and growth, the inevitability of suffer-

ing and healing, are common strands in human experience. Christians affirm these, but we also affirm
something more. Jesus is Lord—raised from the dead for
you and for me to give us new life as we pass through
the valley of the shadow of death.

It was embarrassing to see him that way: a fishmonger
not haggling as he should
but chasing us down our streets
trying to give them away.
Stuff them in our pockets: blues,
great slabs of shark, tiny
rainbowed trout.

Of course it confused the other hawkers.
Stunned, they raised their prices.
No one blamed them. Fear
has its reasons. Eels in short supply
that season he gave away, tucked in widows'
baskets, slipped in children's fists.

Most knew better than to accept them.
When he's come to me
I'd shake my head,
avoid his eyes. I had my system:
lock gaze into vitreous cloud
of eye that floated upside down
in flounder head hanging
at his side.

From the hill even at the last
he was making offers. They drifted
into quays where the other mongers waited,
frightened, hoping for it to be done.

This morning a sudden squall rose
and I caught the smell of him, unexpected
as it all was.

My heart, therefore, is glad, and my spirit rejoices;
my body also shall rest in hope.

The heart is glad both for the promise of new life and for the new freedom to acknowledge death. Human beings will always try to deny death. That is inevitable. But in Jesus we have received a new promise. This promise does away with our need for the elaborate system of defenses each of us constructs to keep ourselves safe from the fact that we are going to die.

When the small child realizes that soon she will be sick to her stomach, she hopes against hope that by lying completely still and swallowing at regular intervals, this too shall pass. It doesn't. Sooner or later there is a mad dash for the bathroom or a great mess on the floor, and then, relief. The clear lesson that it would have been wiser, better, easier to face it and be done with it is not easy to learn until we are mature enough to realize that new life follows that inevitable, embarrassing moment of loss.

❧   ❧   ❧

...The whole time her husband was dying she tried to stay with him and live with him in the present, but something in her wanted him to die, wanted it over with, wanted to get past and around it. Once the future had become clear, she wanted him dead.

It had all gone on for such a long time, too long. Fifteen years ago, he had suffered his first stroke, alone, at home on a Saturday morning. She had gone away for the weekend to help their eldest daughter come home from the hospital with their first grandchild. His stroke occurred a little after nine in the morning. He would have lain there helpless and alone all weekend, and probably would have died, had a neighbor not come by to drop off the book she had borrowed. When he didn't answer the doorbell, she became concerned and called the police.

His recovery took months and was never complete. He could walk only with assistance, and his speech was impaired. Overnight, her very independent husband had become completely dependent for every kind of physical and emotional and financial support. She held a good job, good for supplemental income, but now she must provide the sole support for the family. She soon discovered she was more than able to handle the challenge but when combined with the constant and ever-increasing demands at home, it got to be too much.

At that very time he suddenly seemed to be getting better, the therapy taking hold; she was full of hope. But then he had another stroke, followed by a heart attack. Throughout it was clear he was dying. The slow, steady, downward slide was unstoppable. Therapy, comfortable home surroundings, and great measures of kindness were only stop-gap measures. Death was inevitable. Why didn't he get it over with?

If she allowed such thoughts, then she felt guilty and would make arrangements to go away for a few days, only to return to more guilt. It happened, finally, when she was away on just such a trip. She and the children planned the funeral together and survived with reserve and grace. Now it finally *was* all over, and she was left with memories of fifteen years of never believing she had done everything she ought to have done.

You will show me the path of life;
in your presence there is fullness of joy,
and in your right hand are pleasures for evermore.

The gift we are to be given through death is consistent with our experience through life. Just as we are, we are offered redemption and release. That release means opportunity—life—of a new and different variety. The value we have been given in Christ is offered again, through death, just as we have known it in life. When that awareness dawns, again and again, we are born again to the overwhelming sense that we are loved by none other than God.

No matter how gifted or how ordinary, every single human being is born to face, sooner or later, the reality that he or she is not God. Childhood fancy and our flights of imagination built for us worlds in which we were omnipotent. Only we weren't. We never are. There is nothing inherent in our being that is unusual or remarkable. Not only does death make nonsense of our vain attempts to be like God, but through death there is the fullness of joy, new and everlasting life.

Then, while earth is cast upon the coffin,

The body that has died is now to be committed to the ground, and as this happens it is covered with dirt. Dirt is used, not some more acceptable substitute—rose petals or clean white sand—but earth from the earth that is earthy, "earth to earth, ashes to ashes, dust to dust."

the Celebrant says these words:

In sure and certain hope of the resurrection to eternal life through our Lord Jesus Christ, we commend to Almighty God our sister (brother) N., and we commit her (his) body to the ground; earth to earth, ashes to ashes, dust to dust. The Lord bless her (him) and keep her (him), the Lord make his face to shine upon her (him), and be gracious to her (him), the Lord lift up his countenance upon her (him) and give her (him) peace. Amen.

The Christian understanding of death and resurrection separates sheep from goats, wheat from chaff. We come to the road less traveled. There must be choice.

> The alternatives are simple—terrifyingly simple and clear. To compromise in this matter is to decide; to waver is to decide; to postpone and evade decision is to decide; to hide the matter is to decide. There is no escape. You must say yes or no. There are a thousand ways of saying no; one way of saying yes; and no way of saying anything else.

The choice is ancient: between life and death. We choose life, but the path to life leads through death.

இ   இ   இ

...During the early years of childhood many of the family's doctor friends became part of his daily life. Next door, a medical student; across the street, a neighbor who had just completed residency; his father's legal specialty, Workmen's Compensation, brought him daily professional contact with many physicians who frequently came to the house for conversation or a meal. His conversation with adults had always been encouraged, and much of this talk was with doctors. It was not surprising that the boy developed a strong interest in medicine at an early age. His parents stimulated the interest, and the boy's father arranged for visits to hospitals.

172

Finally, the day came for his first observation of a real operation. Father, son, and doctor friend stood together on an observation balcony directly above the operating room and operating table. Surgeon, anesthesiologist, nurses, interns, medical students, surrounded the table. Eager and enthusiastic as the boy was, the opportunity may not have been good for someone so young—it ended, forever, all interest in medicine. But the memory of the operation never left him.

Surgery was performed on the patient's right leg. Once the surgeon was ready to work, he pointed out to the students an obvious line running from one side of the bone to the other. "A childhood break," he said. "This is where the bone healed after the accident. The line right there, the place where the leg grew back together after the fracture, that's the strongest part of this patient's body. Healing makes us stronger than we were before."

ta.   ta.   ta.

To pull blinds of habit from the eyes,
to see the world without names for the first bright time,
to wander through its mystery, to wonder
at every age and stage, at one with it—
to be alive!
...There is only moving.
We leave ourselves behind.
Our wheels unwind us.
What will we find at the end?
Our selves again, but changed.

ta.   ta.   ta.

Celebrant and people say together standing around the grave.

173

Our Father, who art in heaven,
hallowed be thy Name,
thy kingdom come,
thy will be done,
on earth as it is in heaven.
Give us this day our daily bread.
And forgive us our trespasses,
as we forgive those
who trespass against us.
And lead us not into temptation,
but deliver us from evil.
For thine is the kingdom,
and the power, and the glory,
for ever and ever. Amen.

The Lord's Prayer is the prayer Jesus taught us to pray. Everything about the Lord's Prayer is significant, but in the context of death, more important even than the words of the prayer is our understanding of the act of prayer. There is never a time we do not need to pray, but at death prayer has particular importance. The Lord's Prayer demands that prayer be importunate, honest, and passionate.

Importunate. Jesus placed his statement of the Lord's Prayer in the context of a story of the importunate neighbor, who at midnight needed to borrow three loaves of bread. He knocked and knocked on his friend's door, until the answer came, "Do not bother me; the door is now shut, and my children are with me in bed; I cannot get up and give you anything." The importunate neighbor, however, pays no heed and continues to knock and knock and knock, until finally the friend rises from bed in the middle of the night to help not because the neigh-

174

bor is a friend, but because of his importunity—the persistent repetition of the request.

Whatever we seek through prayer is not as important as the repetition of our request—over and over and over and over again. True prayer is repetitious, even boring, often ungracious, definitely single-minded. There is the sense that it does not take hold until it has worn its own track, created its own place, made its own way.

Honest. Honesty goes with importunity. If one is faithful and repetitious, one speaks from the heart. There are no necessary formulae, although old and repeated words are helpful. At the moment of real need one speaks from the heart—over and over and over and over again. When we do, something happens. It is not always what we want, but something happens. If that something is not what we desire or pray for, we still know that it is God's action in our life for that moment. Prayer has been practiced without ceasing throughout countless generations because it works. It is not like talking alone when asleep, nor can it be compared to the sound of a tree crashing to the ground in a deserted forest. Prayer is our approach to God and God's response.

Passionate. Prayer is passionate, insistent and forthright, the declaration of something that is essential, deeply and directly connected to all you are and have been and will be. Prayer is not the same as casual conversation, as one might report the Dow Jones average for the day or the weather forecast for tomorrow. Prayer is rooted in what we take seriously with no reservations. Most things will not matter a hundred years from now, but those that will are the subject of prayer, the language to, from, with and of God.

❧   ❧   ❧

...Charles said the words of the Lord's Prayer. It was more than just an exercise of rote memory, for he thought about the words as a definition of prayer.

His prayer began with memory, continued as he emptied his mind, allowing and inviting God to sweep over him and carry him in six different directions all at once. Prayer right now was missing Nancy, loving her, all the time knowing that she was right here. Prayer was the culmination of every single moment when Nancy had been there, when the two of them had been gathered together, and when Jesus, just as he had promised, was in the midst of them.

The most real and intense prayer he had ever known happened when he was with one or two others, when they had been gathered together. Most often that other had been Nancy, with whom he had shared so many hours of solitude. He had learned with her and from her and through her what prayer meant. Prayer was one opportunity for the limits of one's own small world to grow. Prayer was not being alone. Prayer was the realization that another person could know what it meant to be inside your own skin. Prayer expanded to include another, others, and always the Other. All of this was possible thanks to Jesus who promised to be in our midst when two or three gather.

> to believe in God
> is to be able to die
> and not to be embarrassed.

Rest eternal grant to her, O Lord;
And let light perpetual shine upon her.

176

Eternal rest is to be free from stress, to know neither haste nor pressure—an everlasting sabbath surrounded by perpetual light, an infusion of radiance that enables growth and vision. This is a description of heaven. None of us has yet been in heaven, but heaven will be consistent with our experience—just as today each of us could say that what we have come to know is usually consistent with what we have learned in the past. So shall it be on our final and longest journey.

The sabbath, every seventh day, is the one day of the week that God at creation directed to be set aside for rest and recreation. "Remember the Sabbath Day and keep it holy" is an injunction that has broad, contemporary application in a culture where stress is considered natural and many forms of addiction are the norm. The sabbath is both essential if we are to fulfill our calling in God's creation and it is also one window through which we may glimpse the fullness of eternal rest, which is heaven.

༂ཨ་   ༂ཨ་   ༂ཨ་

…When he walked into the house late in the day, something was different. The air was charged, but it was meant to be an ordinary Tuesday evening. Muttering to himself that he had no time for anything but eating dinner and getting to work, he headed off for the study to organize the enormous load of work in his briefcase. He would be lucky to get to bed before midnight.

She greeted him as he came down the hall. Without a word she kissed him, took his hand and led him back to the kitchen, where she opened the refrigerator and gathered together the picnic she had just finished preparing. When he started to sputter and fume and complain about the work in his briefcase, she covered his mouth with one hand and laid an index finger over her lips.

"Shh," she said. "Some things are more important than work. Right now you and I are off for a picnic in the park and an evening together. And who knows? We may not even be back until tomorow. You need some time away, and so do I. Don't argue, just come along."

His feet were not all that willing, but he followed. Thank God someone had the sense to break into the never-ending spiral of work and tension.

  ❦ ❦ ❦

Paul Tillich wrote of the contrast between loneliness and solitude. Loneliness, while inevitable, we fear and avoid, for it is part of the pain and isolation of our humaness. Solitude we seek, for in it we become at one with our world, with those around us, with God. When in solitude, we are closest to the God, the One who created and redeemed us and will welcome us into his presence at the very last.

  ❦ ❦ ❦

...He had fallen down a flight of cellar stairs and cracked his head at ten in the morning. By all indications he had stayed there until six in the evening, when a woman friend, invited for supper, climbed in a window and found him. A day later, now in a coma, his face twice its normal size with the bones hidden under the swelling, he lay in the intensive care unit while his daughter tried to talk to him.

178

Not that there was anything to talk about, since he could neither speak nor hear. But that was pretty much the way it always had been. Nothing was very different, except that she was in control. It was not comfortable, as she sat next to his bed and looked at the distorted face of her father, and realized that here at the end, she was in control. Still, she was wistful, and longed to know the person who lay there, all but dead and so unreachable.

Throughout her childhood so many opportunities had been lost, dissolved in all the booze that had removed him. Night after night, day after day, drink had taken him away to some place where she couldn't find him. Had he gone there in fear that nothing real, nothing that involved feeling, passion, or intensity could ever pass between them? And so their household was not a place for feeling, only for performance.

Through many of those years she had wanted to believe that she was different from her family. She still believed it, or tried. But what if she were more like her father and mother than she ever dared to think? Did that mean that parents and children could neither talk nor listen? Sharing secrets was never done with parents. And could it be that if you didn't start sharing yourself with your parents, you would end up not sharing your life with anyone?

She reached over and covered his limp hand with hers. He did not move, not a suggestion of life except the continual rising and falling of his chest, responding to the life support system. Not knowing what to say, she repeated the words of the Lord's Prayer, half out loud. Then she couldn't think of anything else to say, and so she whispered, "Dad. Dad? I love you. I always loved

179

you, and I always will. You loved me too. I'll miss you, just the way I always have."

Her father died that evening at 10:02 P.M.

May his soul, and the souls of all departed,
through the mercy of God, rest in peace. Amen.

Rest comes at long last only through the mercy of God. In rare moments we have known it, not from sleep, not from chemicals, not from travel, not from anything we can do. We have glimpsed it at times, fleeting and shining, as if looking through a key hole into room far larger than any we have seen before. There we shall rest, once upon a time, with all the souls of the departed...through the mercy of God.

· ❧   ❧   ❧

...The call came in mid-morning. Grandfather had died without warning, while taking his morning bath. From their earliest memories the children knew he had been more than a good grandfather; he was everything that three little girls might have hoped for, and they were devoted to him and to their grandmother, Amah. The loss was more than they expected. Nothing like this had ever happened to them before.

The drive to grandmother's house was somber and silent, hardly fitting for a man whose every day with them had been jolly, full of the silly and satirical, laughter that concealed a higher purpose. When they laughed together, they loved together. More, they knew, each of them, no matter how small, that the world was a place of promise.

After everyone had been silent for a long time: "If Baba were here, he would be making us laugh," said the eldest.

And then, from the second, "He would make up a game." Their favorite was Super-Spy. And so the game began.

"Agent 007, reporting for duty."

"0011."

"0013."

Assignments were handed out. Everyone contributed, trying to think Baba's thoughts.

"I know. What kind of toothpaste does Aunt Marlene use? If you're going to answer, you have twenty-five seconds."

"The full name of the brown shoe polish used on all of Baba's shoes."

"What does the subscription to *The Daily News* cost per year?"

"The maker of Baba's watch, and the date he received it."

"Expiration date of the *Time* subscription."

Baba was dead, but this was his game, Baba's treasure hunt. Baba would be gone, but his granddaughters sought his presence.

Did they find it? Yes and no.

They arrived to find the house gripped by death. Amah met them at the kitchen door; her welcome was warm, but her attempt to be cheerful failed. There was little reason—who could blame her? As soon as kisses had been exchanged, agents 007, 0011 and 0013 disappeared to the four corners of the house. Silence. Then shouts, screams, giggles, gales and gales of laugher, until everyone had to lie down. One by one, they again reappeared, on the balcony, around the corner, out of the root cellar. Each with a prize—her answer for Baba's game—for Baba.

Baba was dead, and he would always be dead. Yes, there were reminders of him, everywhere. These grandchildren were his legacy, his temporary immortality, but no one was fooled into thinking that Baba lived on, endlessly, in these delightful memories and funny games. All that had ended, forever, when he expired, this very morning, in the bathtub over there, behind the door no one wanted to open.

Baba was dead, and the three girls knew it. They also knew that when he died, something new was born, different, compelling, important, vital. It was born in their laughter, and it bore them forward.

   ôa. ôa. ôa.

...In his imagination Charles could see himself already leaving the cemetery, driving by himself back to Anne's house, where he and the children would sit together in awkward silence and then share a simple supper around the table he had once made for Nancy.

Supper over, it would be time to drive home, alone, park the car in the garage, take the mail in from the box, as he had done a thousand times. Into the house he would go to turn on the answering machine, and then it would hit him. Nancy was not there. He would do all of those things alone. Days stretched out ahead of him, the letters he would have to write, calls to answer, students to teach, the meals he would cook or not cook. Could he follow her lead, not by dying, but by changing?

It just had to be that her death was an adventure; they were now exploring the unknown. The horizon beckoned to what lay beyond: the unseen and new. Even though she was gone, she had not ceased to be. The days of her life had been a constant testimony to the power of renewal, new life, the ability to be born again in surprising ways, always unforeseen. If this was the way it always had been, it would continue that way both for her and for him.

But the past was over. Really over. All the joy and pain and fulfillment he had known with her, from the love they have been given and then shared, one for the other, was over. In her arms, in her presence, and even in her rage, he had come to know life in its fullness. That was over. Their life together came from God, and it came to him through her—through the miracle of their marriage that gave flesh and blood and passion and pain to the love incarnate in Jesus, and it was over, all over.

What now? What remained for him as she died? He too would die. There would be nothing else for which to live, not when she had gone. He thought what she would say, how she would tell him that this was not the end, never the end. Death had never been the end, not for them. Death had always been a new beginning. The new beginning was always different, but consistent with what had gone before.

What they had known and dreamed and prayed and lived would now be tested, tested as never before, and he would face the test alone, without her constant presence, her wisdom, insight, and love.

No, that was not true. She would be dead, but he would not be alone. He would never be alone.

The God of peace, who brought again from the dead our Lord Jesus Christ, the great Shepherd of the sheep, through the blood of the everlasting covenant: Make you perfect in every good work to do his will, working in you that which is well-pleasing in his sight; through Jesus Christ, to whom be glory for ever and ever. Amen.

❧　　❧　　❧

...Charles stood by the still-open grave. The service was over and he had sent his family on ahead, while he remained alone to complete the ritual of burial. The first few shovels were the most painful. The rocks and clay, residue of a primordial sea, struck the wooden box each time with the hollow sound of a wrecking ball and evoked images of what lay inside, her body that once lived and breathed and loved. Three men dressed in yellow slickers watched. When he finished, they moved forward to replace the sod. He stood for a while before turning to leave. It was over.

As it turned out, it had only just begun.

References

pp. 4-5   Commencement Speech
           Currier House, Harvard College, June 9,
           1988.

p. 21   Samuel Terrien, *Job: Poet of Existence* (Indianapolis, IN: Bobbs-Merrill, 1957), p. 153.

p. 22   Jeremiah 1:5.

p. 40   "A Refusal to Mourn the Death, by Fire, of
           a Child in London" in Dylan Thomas, *Collected Poems* (New York: New Directions,
           1971). Copyright 1945 by the Trustees for
           the Copyrights of Dylan Thomas. Reprinted by permission of New Directions
           Publishing Corporation. U. S. rights; for
           Canadian and British rights, refer to David
           Higham Associates, Ltd., 5-8 Lower John
           Street, Golden Square, London W1R 4HA,
           England.

p. 43   Exodus 14:11-12.

pp. 43-44 A. A. Milne, *The World of Pooh* (New York:
           E. P. Dutton, 1975), pp. 307-314.

p. 46   John Cheever, "Expelled" in *The New Republic* (19-26 June 1982):32-36.

p. 54   Judith Guest, *Ordinary People* (New York: Ballantine, 1976), pp. 1-2.

p. 60   Hymn 689, The Hymnal 1982.

pp. 82-83   Romans 6:5.

p. 102   Kenneth Fearing, "Requiem" in *Collected Poems* (New York: Random House, 1936). Copyright 1936, 1964 by Kenneth Fearing. Reprinted by permission of Russell and Volkening as agents for the author.

p. 103   Emily Dickinson, "A Death Blow Is a Life Blow to Some" in *The Complete Poems of Emily Dickinson* (Boston: Little Brown, 1960).

p. 105   Thomas Wolfe, *Look Homeward Angel* (New York: Scribner's, 1929), p. 502.

p. 108   Romans 6:23.

p. 112   *The New Mexican*, August 7, 1989: A-5.

pp. 112-113   Helmut Gollwitzer, Kathe Kuhn, Reinhold Schneider, eds., *Dying We Live* (New York: Pantheon, 1956), pp. 282-285.

p. 117   John 21:9-12.

pp. 121-122   Wolfe, *Look Homeward Angel*, frontispiece.

pp. 122   Philip Larkin, "Aubade" in *Collected Poems* (New York: Farrar, Straus & Giroux, 1989). Copyright 1988, 1989 by the Estate of Philip Larkin. Reprinted by permission of Farrar, Straus & Giroux, Inc.

p. 123   Hymn 345, The Hymnal 1982.

p. 124   John 12:24.

p. 125   John Marquand, *Point of No Return* (Boston: Little Brown, 1949), pp. 440-441.

p. 126   Luke 24:13-15, 28-31a.

pp. 132   Edward Carpenter, "Towards Democracy" in Dorothy Berkely Phillips, ed., *The Choice Is Always Ours* (New York: Harper & Row, 1948), p. 43.

p. 137   John 6:35.

p. 143   Hymn 661, The Hymnal 1982.

p. 140   Chilson H. Leonard, "Of Things Unseen," *In Touch With Space* (Exeter, NH: The Phillips Exeter Academy Press, 1967), pp. 28-29.

p. 146   1 John 4:16.

p. 158   Matthew 25:34-36.

p. 159 Matthew 10:42.

p. 160 Revelation 21:1-4.

p. 168 Littlepage Smith, "Lent." Unpublished. Used by permission.

p. 172 Gregory Vlastos, "The Religious Way" in Phillips, ed., *The Choice Is Always Ours.*

p. 173 Alastair Reid, *To Be Alive!* (New York: Macmillan, 1966), pp. 1, 33.

pp. 174-175 Luke 11:1-10.

p. 176 Joseph Pintauro, *To Believe in God* (New York: Harper & Row, 1968), p. 65.

p. 178 Paul Tillich, "Loneliness and Solitude" in *The Eternal Now* (New York: Charles Scribner's Sons, 1963), pp. 15-25.